BWB Texts

Short books on big subjects from great New Zealand writers

Christchurch Ruptures

KATIE PICKLES

Published in 2016 by Bridget Williams Books Limited, PO Box 12474, Wellington 6144, New Zealand, www.bwb.co.nz, info@bwb.co.nz.

ISBN 9780908321292 (Paperback), ISBN 9780908321308 (EPUB),
ISBN 9780908321315 (KINDLE), ISBN 9780908321322 (PDF),
ISTC A0220150000000FB
DOI http://dx.doi.org/10.7810/9780908321292

A catalogue record for this book is available from the National Library of New Zealand. Kei te pātenga raraunga o Te Puna Mātauranga o Aotearoa te whakarārangi o tēnei pukapuka

Acknowledgements
The publisher acknowledges the ongoing support provided by the Bridget Williams Books Publishing Trust and Creative New Zealand.

creative nz
ARTS COUNCIL OF NEW ZEALAND TOI AOTEAROA

Publisher: Tom Rennie
Editors: Jane Parkin and Nancy Swarbrick
Cover and internal design: Base Two
Typesetter: Tina Delceg
Printer: Printlink, Wellington

CONTENTS

THE RUPTURE

On 22 February 2011 Christchurch and surrounding districts were hit by a magnitude 6.3 earthquake that was an aftershock from a 4 September 2010 magnitude 7.1 quake. Put together with thousands of aftershocks, this series of events comprises the 'Canterbury earthquakes of 2010 and 2011', a disaster unprecedented in scale and cost in New Zealand. In February 2011, 185 people lost their lives and 6,600 were seriously injured. The long series of physical aftershocks carries on and the local, national and global implications of Canterbury's loss continue to reverberate. The Canterbury earthquakes of 2010 and 2011 have forced an abrupt rupture from the past and Christchurch is in the spotlight as a place forced to look to the future in unique and urgent ways. The earthquakes have taken lives and homes and assaulted and destroyed senses of belonging. This book will argue that they have also have fractured pathways to remembering the past.

With an historian's perspective, *Christchurch Ruptures* delves into the earthquakes and their aftermath; then goes back into the history of Christchurch, filling in the complexities of the past so as to suggest ways of achieving a fresh, open-minded and harmonious present and future. According to historian Raphael Samuel, history is a living practice, and it is constantly reassessed in the world around us; that is, we conjure historical fictions to make sense of our everyday lives.[1] As this book shows, this is a useful way of considering history-making at Christchurch's moment of rupture. The past can be considered as a text that is being rapidly written and rewritten, or a canvas with an ever-changing composition. Faced with loss and grief, people seek comfort in the past and return to and retell their histories. Tales of past people and places can form new nostalgic narratives that simplify and celebrate history.

Each chapter of this book analyses an area of rupture concerning landscape, people, heritage, culture and politics. These areas are connected through a contest over place-making and hegemony. Running through the chapters are the often competing interests of fear, division, vision and pragmatism that co-exist at a moment when the past abruptly meets the future. Through the five ruptures, the book identifies some of the major ways in which the city has changed, with the purpose of thinking beyond the earthquakes and into the future through understanding of the past.

When a large event happens, there is a risk that the one traumatic moment becomes the sum total of the history of that place. In Christchurch's case, it took an awful disaster for the city to become world-famous. With the focus on the immediate aftermath, at exactly the time when a strong awareness of the past is acutely needed in order to cope with the present and to plan for the future, it is instead at risk of being hidden and forgotten. David Lowenthal has argued that the past allows us to make sense of the present, and that it is important to question how some aspects of the past become celebrated while others are expunged, as new generations reshape their stories in line with current needs.[2] Recognising these risks, the objective of *Christchurch Ruptures* is to work through the clichés that can accompany times of change, and in light of what has changed, to grapple with what Christchurch was before 2010 and consider what it might become. Through the identified ruptures this book recovers aspects of Christchurch's economic, social, cultural and political history that provide both comfort and challenge in times of upheaval, and analyses them so that they might usefully inform the rebuilding of the city.

The earthquakes have exposed major components in the history of Christchurch, such as the dominant Anglican tradition and Englishness, the denial of a Māori past, and the environmental pitfalls of building a city on a swamp. The book argues that these features need to be looked at anew and that it is unhelpful and inaccurate to cling to an imagined city, or attempt to rebuild, restore and regenerate aspects of the past that were long gone before the earth moved. Rather, mindful of the past, it is important to consolidate in the present and embrace the future. It is here that Christchurch's recovery story will be useful globally as well as locally and nationally.

An important theme underlying the ruptures identified in this book is the significance of the break from the colonial past. Prior to the earthquakes, Christchurch was located as a systematically planned new-world city on the edge of the British Empire. A common dominant narrative asserted that the city and province were the confident outcome of a colonising project inspired by Edward Gibbon Wakefield and the New Zealand Company.[3] But as the Canterbury earthquakes have shown, geological uncertainty has rendered the ideas and practice of colonialism severely compromised. Significantly, the Canterbury earthquakes have necessitated a 'postcolonial moment' where the past is rethought at a time of acute vulnerability that is in contrast to past colonial confidence. Postcolonialism is a broad term with many, often contradictory meanings, and different emphases in various regions of the world. In New Zealand, redress for Māori land loss, combined with the social, political, cultural and economic implications of Treaty of Waitangi claims, mean that the environment is necessarily central in postcolonial scholarship.[4] Adding a layer to this environmental emphasis is New Zealand's identity as a place where settlers from Europe were both colonisers and the colonised, seeking to create a 'second world' or a 'Better Britain' that mimicked the imperial centre.[5] The Canterbury earthquakes have naturally given rise to questions about the wisdom of continuing to take the lead from European concepts of order and progress. Instead, the concept of 'provincialising Europe'; that is, giving preference to local environments and the people who inhabit them, is proposed.[6] For New Zealand, Eric Pawson has explicitly referred to 'postcolonial' being usefully considered as 'a continuous engagement with the lasting effects of colonialism'.[7] Gradual devolution away from Britain, rather than revolution, suits the New Zealand nation.[8]

This book builds upon the important work of Jane M. Jacobs, who in *Edge of Empire: Post-*

colonialism and the City, demonstrated how British imperialism 'carved its way through space: possessing and ordering territories across the globe'. Furthermore, as her work shows, the 'spatial legacy' of empire 'lingers in the present and shapes the nature of postcolonial futures'.[9] It is a legacy that involves the interconnection of hegemony, landscape and culture, and forms a major theme in the ruptures examined in this book. Such an approach is common in cultural geography, where places are considered as constructed texts.[10] A critique of dominant colonial ways of seeing the environment has long existed in the New Zealand context, with the focus often on rural areas.[11] More generally, Simon Schama has demonstrated how culture is infused in landscapes, existing in what may be considered unlikely and unrecognised places.[12]

In *The Villa at the Edge of the Empire: One Hundred Ways to Read a City*, Fiona Farrell emphasises the importance of the neo-liberal political context in which the Canterbury earthquakes occurred. She writes, 'The laboratory is humming, and in the great experiment, Christchurch, shaken to its core, stripped back to bare essentials, lies cracked and open in the petri dish beneath the wide arc of the Canterbury sky'.[13] 'Market-led' philosophies, present before the earthquakes, have gained momentum since 2011 and have resulted in job losses, school closures and the destruction of communities. Shortly before the earthquakes, in March 2010, local democracy was suspended when central government sacked fourteen elected Canterbury Regional Council (Environment Canterbury) councillors and replaced them with seven commissioners, chaired by Dame Margaret Bazley. Into that context came the 2011 Canterbury Earthquake Regional Authority (CERA), endowed with extensive powers to rebuild the city. The earthquakes have added to the suspension of democracy, and have brought pre-quake patterns into sharp relief.

Just as the Canterbury earthquakes have generated a charged political atmosphere, so too should power relations in past landscapes be considered dynamic and often complicated. In the twentieth century Antonio Gramsci and Raymond Williams worked on the concept of dynamic hegemony in civil societies. Williams is particularly useful because of his concern with culture. He argues that 'the reality of cultural process must then always include the efforts and contributions of those who are in one way or another outside or at the edge of the terms of the specific hegemony'. This is a theme explored through the chapters of *Christchurch Ruptures*; for example, in the interplay between the supposedly oppositional 'conservative' and 'radical' citizens, and the contact between Māori and Pākehā. Understanding that domination is subject to continual change is particularly useful in post-quake Christchurch.[14] It gives citizens hope to participate in and influence their local communities in a context where central government's establishment of CERA to coordinate the post-quake recovery effort set the tone of national governance, supported by the latest trends in global capitalism, overriding local voices.

This book identifies and examines aspects of Christchurch city's history that have ruptured during the Canterbury earthquakes. The focus is on the connection between people and their environments, and the dynamic workings of landscape, culture and hegemony: from Māori–Pākehā race relations, to neo-Gothic sensibilities, to 'the People's Republic of Christchurch', to the debate over the future of the Anglican cathedral. Various aspects of the city's social, cultural, political and environmental history are traversed as relevant to understanding how the city has changed. Overall, the ruptures are identified to assist thinking about the present and planning for the future.

1. LANDSCAPE

When Christchurch's built and natural landscape ruptured during the Canterbury earthquakes, so too did its history and future. Simon Schama writes that because expressions of culture and belief are evident in the landscape, 'even the landscapes that we suppose to be most free of our culture may turn out, on closer inspection, to be its product'.[1] The earthquakes laid bare the acute connections between physical and built environments and the social structures that breathed life into them. During a bleak time involving the tragic loss of life and the destruction of homes, neighbourhoods, livelihoods, hopes and dreams, landscapes of all persuasions ruptured.

Considering a theme that is developed throughout this book, this chapter is concerned with the connection between Christchurch's spatial structure (the place), and its social structure (the people) as manifested together in landscapes.[2] It analyses broken and changed landscapes by reading them as living historical texts in which meaning is created. At times of shocking and visible loss, reinvention of the past occurs in numerous ways. For Christchurch, such recasting has been partly a reaction to the significant rupture of predominant colonial narratives that characterised the city as a place with deep roots in the 'old world' and that downplayed the city's physical location. Other places and peoples have often been emulated throughout Christchurch's colonial history. As this chapter shows, the scramble to regroup and move forward involves reconfiguring history by drawing upon particular memory markers and frames of reference, both local and distant (such as London during the Blitz). As Christchurch's rupture confirms, memories are highly selective, always partial, and constantly being formed and reformed.

Post-quake attempts to come to terms with abrupt change, regroup and rebuild can still downplay the importance of Christchurch's geographic location. Relic imperial attitudes of conquest and settlement, and the impulse to perpetuate old-world landscapes, remain. Recognition that the city, and indeed New Zealand, is located astride the colliding Pacific and Australian tectonic plates and is part of the Pacific Ring of Fire should be paramount in decision-making about the city's future. The time for creating a nostalgic small colonial city that belongs elsewhere is over.

During Christchurch's post-quake 'clean-up', a wholesale demolition of history took place. Thousands of tonnes of rubble were removed, taken to rubbish dumps and buried. Building materials finely crafted into places imbued with memory and identity over many years, including shops, homes and hotels, were disassembled and removed. Not all rubble, however, was equal. On 22 February, the effigy of the city's founding father and Director of the Canterbury Association, John Robert Godley, was shaken off its pedestal after 143 years standing in Cathedral Square. A statue of early provincial superintendent William Rolleston fell backwards off its plinth outside Canterbury Museum on Rolleston Avenue, to lie beheaded by the forces of nature. British imperial adventurer Captain Robert Falcon Scott's likeness fell too. It was located on the corner of Oxford Terrace and Worcester Street, between Cathedral Square and Canterbury Museum. Journalist Charlie Gates wrote of these statues as symbols of 'despair and fear'.[3] Unlike many other items, however, these and other sculptures commissioned and placed by colonial settlers were rescued and stored away as

Pākehā treasures. These notable statues can be read as texts of Christchurch's colonial past – a past that had literally broken. Their destruction symbolises the end of a colonial era in Christchurch.

Placed in global context, the felling of these Christchurch works of art recalls images of statues of former leaders such as Saddam Hussein and Joseph Stalin being eagerly pulled down by societies erasing the old and advancing the new. Politically closer to home, statues that evoke colonisation have been removed in some former colonies of the British Empire. In India, statues of Queen Victoria have been put in storage. More dramatically, in 1963 in Canada, the Front de Libération du Québec blew the head off a Queen Victoria statue in Québec City, making clear its desire to break from the past.[4] The head has remained detached in the decades since, even appearing as a museum exhibit, a political relic from the past. Meanwhile, in Whanganui's Moutoa Gardens (Pakaitore), a site of contested memorialisation, a statue of local newspaper editor and Premier of New Zealand, John Ballance, was beheaded and damaged beyond repair during an occupation by Whanganui Māori in 1995.[5] In Auckland's Albert Park, the statue of Sir George Grey has been decapitated many times.[6]

The cause of such destruction in Christchurch was different. Importantly, in a city that has often rushed to cultivate an 'English' identity, it took an environmental event to topple memorials – and to shunt society off its colonial tracks. The change to Christchurch's identity was uncontrollably led from under the earth. Not all of the city's statues fell over, but the inner-city zone they occupied was permanently ruptured.

In drawing up new plans for the post-quake city, there are questions about the place of these memorials. In the meantime, located in a container in the destroyed Cashel Mall, Canterbury Museum's 'Quake City' exhibition has displayed 'iconic objects' from Christchurch's pre-quake landscape as history.[7] Suggesting that Christchurch should carry on regardless, Public Art Advisory Group chair Anthony Wright said, 'It is a very chilling kind of blow when you see our forebears and founders falling, but here is a fantastic opportunity for them to rise again.'[8] But Jenny May's pre-earthquake work on the Godley Statue and the plot it stood on revealed that the site was subject to dissatisfaction and dispute. May questioned the relevance of focusing solely on Godley in that central place, pointing out that women and children were also vital in systematic colonisation.[9] In 2015, however, Godley's statue was reinstated in Cathedral Square. As Charles Cole has noted: 'It is ... possible that Godley may once again be left standing, watching and waiting for his cathedral to be built.'[10]

Until 22 February 2011, Christchurch enjoyed one of the tidiest colonial histories in the world. Colonialism is a concept used in many ways, but for our purposes it is a process whereby people from dominant territories, usually expanding empires, left their familiar old world and migrated to settle in a new place. Indigenous peoples were expected to make way for progress, while settlers were expected to reproduce their old society in new and improved form. This meant importing attitudes that confidently asserted superiority over local knowledge. A great deal of migration now is voluntary, as people move in search of better opportunities for themselves and their families. In the eighteenth and nineteenth centuries movement to parts of the British Empire was often involuntary, with the Highland Clearances, the Irish Famine and transportation to Australia being examples of circumstances forcing migration.

The Canterbury Association, by contrast, was the brainchild of Edward Gibbon Wakefield, whose dream was to colonise the area systematically with a mix of classes in a Church of England settlement.[11] The appropriately named Godley actualised the vision, in 1848 forming the Canterbury Association with Wakefield.[12] The Canterbury Association's first choice of a place for settlement was Wairarapa, but Māori resistance to selling land and the absence of a decent harbour led to a shift south.[13] In the same year, without struggle and with a number of guaranteed reserves and privileges (see Chapter 2), the region's major iwi, Ngāi Tahu, sold a large tract of land stretching from Kaiapoi to Otago, opening the way for settlement. Those who had been living on the Canterbury Plains for hundreds of years were clearly on the margins of the proposed settlement. The rhythms of pre-contact life were disrupted permanently in the name of progress and betterment, for settlers as well as Māori.[14]

The experienced Captain Joseph Thomas was commissioned to choose a site for the new settlement and survey the land in preparation for the arrival of the legendary 'first four ships' of settlers in 1850. Christchurch was planned according to the principles of systematic colonisation. The grid shape of the city was stamped onto the landscape with a confident laying of foundations and many colonial hopes and dreams for the future.[15] There was some attention to the local geography. Surveyors were aware that the swampy nature of coastal Canterbury was unsuited to urban development. For many years, schoolchildren were taught that the site chosen for Christchurch was the first reasonably dry and slightly elevated area handy to the limits of boat navigation on the Heathcote and Avon rivers, and that Thomas's 'decision was to be vindicated as the settlement progressed'.[16]

Unfortunately, relying largely upon experience elsewhere in the world, the colonists had insufficient knowledge to understand the havoc that would be caused by liquefaction following major earthquakes. On the contrary, as products of their times, they believed that nature could be controlled and conquered. So Christchurch became 'the city on the swamp', with all the attendant problems of ill health, smog and difficulties with drainage. In winter low-lying parts of the city flooded, and the ponds left behind turned stagnant in the summer. In the 1870s Christchurch had a reputation as New Zealand's unhealthiest town, with death from bacterial diseases such as typhoid fever and influenza twice the national average.[17] Through most of the twentieth century, in winter months chimney smoke combined with fog to produce high levels of the toxic pollutant 'smog'.

With the benefit of hindsight it is all too easy to question the city's location. But people were thinking with a mindset of confidence, faith in progress and hope. And when earthquakes happened, nature could be seen to be at fault, rather than human behaviour. Human control and mastery of the earth would carry on regardless – an optimism that echoes in the current clearing of Christchurch city centre and rebuilding 'from scratch'. As Chapter 5 reveals, new suburbs are already being pegged out on previously swampy sites, very close to fault lines.

A feature of colonial settlement was to start with a blank slate, leaving out the indigenous past. Captain Thomas and his assistant Edward Jollie set about naming the grid-patterned streets with familiar reference points. Firmly identifying Christchurch as a part of the British Empire, the street names – Durham, Armagh, St Asaph, Montreal and Madras – were taken from bishoprics in England, Ireland, Wales and other colonies. Perhaps the most potent symbol of the imperial enterprise was the Anglican cathedral. A long time in the planning, the main building was ready in 1881 and provided the iconic central point for colonial Christchurch. Indeed, popular opinion has held that the city is named after this building, when in reality Godley chose the name in remembrance of Christ Church, his old college at Oxford University.

The 'four avenues' that became the boundary of the inner-city disaster zone were named after the city's first four superintendents during the period of provincial government: James Edward FitzGerald, William Sefton Moorhouse, Samuel Bealey and William Rolleston. As a part of their shared vision, these men accepted ideals of urban design based on European architecture and had little reason to believe that the built environment in New Zealand would be any different. In 1865 the Provincial Council Chambers, constructed from stone quarried at Halswell, were erected proudly in place of wooden buildings – a grand and ambitious project inspired by the old world. Writing in 1948, Patricia Morrison captures the sentiment:

> The evolution of Christchurch was the work of men, the results of their reaction to circumstances and events, and the history of the establishment of institutions into which they put their energy, toil of body and brain and their idealism. And these are the stuff of which history is made. The story of man's achievements and failures whether on a greater or lesser scale is never negligible if on that work there are founded the lives and institutions of men of to-day.[18]

The Canterbury earthquakes have fractured much of Christchurch's visible colonial heritage, turning the land located within the four avenues into a wasteland associated with death and destruction. Much of the distinctive Gothic revival architecture that united Christchurch with other British settlements of the same era in Australia, Canada, India and Britain is severely damaged. Led especially by the Anglican Church, a transnational 'Imperial Gothic' landscape developed. The many churches and cathedrals built in the mid-nineteenth century around the British world were, as G. A. Bremner puts it, about 'propriety and truth' and 'transplanting the faith'.[19] As modern local knowledge about the danger of earthquakes emerged, there were attempts in Christchurch by heritage advocates to preserve these buildings, following best practices towards historic places applied in the old world. For example, the Canterbury Provincial Chambers building was strengthened, and the former site of the University of Canterbury was made into an Arts Centre.

In 2011, shortly after the Canterbury earthquakes, Bruce Ansley wrote *Christchurch Heritage: A Celebration of Lost Buildings and Streetscapes*. The book claimed to be:

> ... a true celebration of Christchurch the way it used to be, and it contains a message of hope – if the city authorities go about the task of rebuilding with the courage, determination and style of their forebears 150 years before, then perhaps in the future people might be celebrating their new heritage with the same depth of emotion as this generation mourns the loss of the old.[20]

Amidst the nostalgia for post-quake heritage, there was a glossing-over of the reality that the city had been knocking down its heritage buildings for a long time. As John Wilson recorded in 1984, very few buildings from the mid-nineteenth century survived.[21] Ten years later, the Aulsebrooks factory, Addington railway workshops and the Edmonds 'Sure to Rise' factory building became further notable examples of 'lost Christchurch.' Following the earthquakes, Wilson, more realistically than Ansley, lamented the large number of buildings he believed were demolished unnecessarily, adding, 'But really, the city has gone and there is no option but grief.' For Wilson, a building 'has an almost spiritual aspect, retaining all that has occurred within its walls. It's not an easy concept to express.'[22]

Christchurch's colonial landscape was in fact always in transition, constantly being made and remade. Many of its people had ignored the city's colonial past until the earthquakes brought it back into focus. Between June and October 2011, *Reconstruction: Conversations on a City*, an aptly titled assemblage of drawings, paintings, photographs, plans, maps and prints from libraries and archives around the country, with written commentaries on free-standing panels, formed an exhibition curated by Christchurch Art Gallery's Ken Hall.[23] The exhibition literally recollected key landscapes from Christchurch's past and presented and analysed them. Importantly, the exhibition presented Christchurch sites alongside images of old European relics. The subtext was that if not for the earthquakes, after centuries of permanence Christchurch's buildings would have crumbled into wondrous ruins. In truth, the earthquakes reinforced knowledge that without careful preservation, old buildings become dangerous earthquake risks. New legislation and the inspection of buildings nationwide in the wake of the Canterbury earthquakes demonstrate a fresh awareness of the consequences of living in an earthquake zone.

Early images of Christchurch in *Reconstruction: Conversations on a City* capture the city rising out of the swamp, and there is the implication that this is what it should do for a second time. Yet caution is needed, as post-quake flooding has warned. The water table has changed; areas of the city are sodden and prone to flood.

The panels portrayed in the *Reconstruction: Conversations on a City* exhibition showed how the neo-Gothic styles of the old world had been copied in the new. For example, following a belief that a solid education demanded solid environments copied from Britain's best, Christchurch's colonists built impressive college and school buildings. Similarly, Venetian style buildings, popular for inner-city shops and offices, demonstrated a gaze towards Europe rather than the Asia–Pacific region. Copying and mimicking institutions and styles were the order of the day.

As Christchurch rises, there is the opportunity to assess the finished past and to confidently and safely build anew. There is also the chance to defy global uniformity and rebuild in a unique

Christchurch style. Reading buildings in the landscape as texts shows how dreams, beliefs and values find expression in the built environment. As this chapter demonstrates, Christchurch's architectural style strongly evokes the colonial past. Drawing upon myths and memories of what Christchurch was, the exhibition *Reconstruction: Conversations on a City* featured the A frame huts that were a very fleeting and temporary part of Christchurch's settlement history. The memory of the huts has been preserved and passed on through generations. In a way, the earthquakes have revived experiences of first settlement – living in temporary tents and huts, dealing with transience and uncertainty, watching homes succumbing to the environment – and forced people to emulate the pioneer spirit. The way to a new start is to reject the imperial mentality of conquering the environment, and instead to work with the surrounds.

In the past the city constantly renewed itself and in reality was very keen to demolish yesterday's buildings. Stone proved more permanent, as wood was more of a fire risk. In contrast to late twentieth-century heritage advocates, pragmatic settlers often favoured replacing buildings. One of the huge difficulties faced when considering preservation of buildings is that it is now known that the badly maintained and old can be deadly dangerous.[24] Ironically, only after disaster is there now much nostalgia and amongst some a sense of loss; for others, there is a sense of relief, cleansing and a clean slate.

Christchurch's railway stations illustrate the pre-quake complex layers of the city. The first wooden station was replaced in the early 1880s by a stone station in modern and Venetian Gothic style. The now-demolished modernist station was planned in the 1930s, but did not open until 1960. The clock on its red brick tower stood still after 4 September 2010 – the past ruptured – serving as a powerful sign that it is not possible to turn back the clock, however strong the yearning.

At Christchurch's time of rupture, plenty of culturally-influenced theories concerning colonial landscapes emerged. Some of these framed the earthquakes as an enemy to be reckoned with, defeated and overcome, rather than as an environmental hazard to be accommodated and respected. In some viewpoints there is little difference in response between natural disasters and human-induced disasters such as warfare.

Perpetuating the ties between London and New Zealand,[25] a suite of historical and cultural reference points have emerged, such as the 'keep calm and carry on' slogan from London's Blitz. The likeness between early twenty-first-century earthquake-ravaged Christchurch and mid-twentieth-century bombed London is explicit in some of these. An article in the *Star* in 2014 drew on interviews with two Christchurch women who were girls in London during the Blitz. One woman thought that the quakes were worse than the bombings, but the other said she feared the bombings more. Both agreed that the Canterbury earthquakes had triggered their memories of the Blitz.[26] Part of the resonance here concerns the similar frame of mind that war and disasters can engender: citizens develop resilience to overcome adversity. But in choosing London and a particular web of historical moments and cityscapes as reference points, care must be taken that this is not at the expense of thinking locally, and in the twenty-first century. Making such connections can also highlight cultural biases and on-going preferences that continue to privilege an imagined Europe over environmentally similar, strategically useful, yet culturally distant places such as Japan. Kobe's 1995 earthquake and its rebuild provide useful lessons to draw upon.[27] The devastating Japanese Fukushima earthquakes of April 2011 also have a humbling similarity to Christchurch's experience. Yet the perceived need to think historically and to seek out European frames of reference evokes the remnants of a colonial past all the more strongly.[28]

In addition to London during the Blitz, two other European landscapes that came to people's minds after Christchurch ruptured, especially for the older generations, were the cities of Coventry and Dresden. These two cities suffered devastating bombing during the Second World War, resulting in large loss of life. Significantly at the time, it was opposing forces who destroyed each place: the German Luftwaffe hit Coventry, and the British Royal Air Force hit Dresden. Many years after these events, who was responsible has become less important than what was lost. Similarly, in early twenty-first-century Christchurch it is the effect on the landscape that is now important, and cultural outcomes are more significant than outmoded geopolitics. The cathedrals located in the centre of both Coventry and Dresden were very badly damaged. As discussed in Chapter 5, Christchurch's Anglican cathedral has become a symbol of hope for the city, and heritage advocates have looked to Coventry and Dresden as useful reference points. The cities would be of little interest had they turned their cathedral site into a shopping mall, or a carpark (as was suggested for Dresden). Instead they are inspirational for those seeking to either restore the cathedral, as in the case of Dresden, or to leave it as a ruined shell and rebuild a new cathedral next to it, as in the case of Coventry.

What is useful in the examples of Coventry and Dresden in twenty-first-century Christchurch is the message of reconciliation, peace and harmony that both sites carry with them. The philosophy behind Dresden's Frauenkirche is that it should be a landmark that evokes and encourages reconciliation between former warring enemies. In the case of Coventry, the rebuilding of a new modern cathedral next to the old ruins was not intended as an act of defiance, but as a sign of faith, trust and hope for the future of the world. In tapping into this spirit of Coventry and Dresden, it is also important for Christchurch to respect the forces of nature and improve upon the previous record of attempting to tame and control them. Distant cultural frames of reference need to be grounded in local reality.

But is Christchurch poised to pick up on the transcendental messages of Coventry and Dresden and move to an enlightened age of living in and with its environment? On the contrary, it is the 9/11 attitude of 'carrying on regardless' that has become an important post-quake reference point for many Cantabrians. The attack on New York's World Trade Centre in September 2001 was for many the defining moment of the first decade of the twentieth century. And more than any other event, the Canterbury earthquakes have occurred in its shadow. Even prior to the quakes, a firefighters' memorial using steel from the destroyed twin towers appeared in Christchurch in 2002 at the time of the World Firefighters' Games. Honouring firefighters around the world, the memorial symbolised a 9/11 ethos that was ready and waiting to be tapped into. A witness giving testimony before the Canterbury Earthquakes Royal Commission recalled that watching the horrific collapse of the CTV Building was as terrifying as watching the twin towers fall. 'White Lights of Hope', organised by Janine Morrell-Gunn and Jason Gunn, was inspired by New York's 'Tribute in Light', consisting of two blue memorial lights shining upwards from where the towers had stood. Christchurch's white lights were turned on a year after the earthquake of 4 September 2010 and shone until 23 February 2012, the day after the one-year anniversary of the February 2011 earthquake. New Zealanders around the country were asked to shine lights up to the sky to show solidarity and support at the same time as the Christchurch lights were turned on. It was too unsafe to do so, but Morrell-Gunn had plans for the lights to come out of the Anglican cathedral itself, characterising it as Christchurch's equivalent of the twin towers. Evoking the overcoming of terror and rebuilding after destruction, the lights in both Christchurch and New York were intended as symbols of hope.

The Canterbury earthquakes ruptured the past, literally forcing new plans to be made for the city. There is the opportunity to reconsider the past and create a safe, sustainable future. In August 2011 architect Perry T. Royal made comments supporting a new city plan that would regenerate a Māori past. He considered that the city precinct was first important to the Waitaha people, and later Ngāi Tahu, as the 'centre of their rohe [territory], together with the river providing the central focus for the people, all transportation, navigation, commercial trading and food gathering activities', and claimed that it 'has been the ecological "vein" nourishing this whole area'. His vision for a new city centre included strengthening and widening the river corridor as a functional ecological and recreational precinct.[29]

One year on from the earthquakes, journalist Martin van Beynen wrote that 'comparisons are often misleading' but nonetheless pondered how Christchurch would look on the tenth anniversary of the earthquakes:

> Will the currently dead spaces of the central city be transformed into cleverly designed, well-built and distinctive areas, full of life and vigour, or will we be staring at desolate carparks and warehouse-like shops? Will we have reclaimed our image as the garden city where cyclists and pedestrians rule or will we be a transit point between Wellington and the lower South Island?[30]

At a time of making way for the fresh and new it is important to consider what has changed about Christchurch, what is best left in the past, and what should be recovered. The earthquake of 22 February 2011 was a postcolonial moment mostly for Christchurch, but it also set off warning bells at a national level about future-proofing the relationship with the environment. This necessitates questioning previous colonial practices and attitudes, the remnants of which abound in the landscape.

2. PEOPLE

There is no term of endearment or official name for a person from Christchurch. There is no 'Christchurcher' or 'smog-dweller'. Rather 'Cantabrian' is the label of choice, suggesting a firm and unbreakable bond between city and surrounding region. Yet Christchurch people have distinct identities. So who were the people of Christchurch dominating narratives prior to the earthquakes of 2010 and 2011? Some individuals and groups of people came to influence the way Christchurch people were characterised. Were these people from the highest social strata of society? How have the earthquakes ruptured the way Christchurch people are perceived? Have the earthquakes challenged the traditional settler stories of the Deans brothers and the first four ships? This chapter juxtaposes the dominant narratives of long-term inhabitants of Christchurch with those of new, post-quake migrants, and with Ngāi Tahu's stories. Ngai Tahu's evolving relationship with the city spans past exclusion and struggle, post-Treaty settlement, rapid growth and post-quake recovery. While on the face of it Christchurch appears to have experienced separate class and ethnic mythologies, there was always cultural contact. The earthquakes have encouraged interaction, providing more opportunity to recognise past cultural encounters and to promote working together in the present and future.

The Canterbury earthquakes have forced Christchurch to rebuild. As a result, construction has boomed. In 2013, one in eight adults in paid work in Christchurch was in the construction industry, and between 2006 and 2013 construction replaced manufacturing as the most common industry.[1] The number of technicians and trades workers in greater Christchurch increased 6.9 per cent between 2006 and 2013; over the same period nationally, there was a 5.8 per cent decrease. The demographic of today's 'Wild East town' is overwhelmingly masculine, reminiscent of the settlement populated by labourers and tradesmen that was established by the Canterbury Association in the 1850s. Of the 1,947 additional technicians and trades workers in 2013, only sixty-six were female. Some women are bravely entering the construction industry, but there has been only a very slight increase, from 13.1 per cent in 2006 (2,112 women) to 14.5 per cent (3,735 women) in greater Christchurch following the earthquake.[2] The boom in women's employment during the rebuild occurred with an influx of prostitutes to the city; an observer noted that 'Christchurch could soon resemble a gold mining frontier town.'[3]

To perform the required labour in the post-quake rebuild, a new wave of migrants has moved to the city, precipitating a demographic rupture – and an unprecedented discussion of ethnicity. In 2013 Immigration Minister Michael Woodhouse said 'there is no doubt in my mind that the rebuild is going to require a significant number of migrant labourers', and he predicted that almost half of the estimated 35,000 workers needed for the rebuild could come from overseas. Woodhouse thought that the city would become 'a pretty cosmopolitan place probably for the next 15 years'.[4] As one commentator put it: 'as the Christchurch rebuild draws workers from around the world, the city's demographics as well as its buildings look set to change'.[5] There has indeed been a net inflow of international migrants to the Canterbury region since 2012. In the last six months of that year, 4,000 people moved to the region, at an average of twenty-five people per day. Some of these overseas workers will have come to the city on working holiday visas to take up jobs in the reconstruction effort.[6]

While a change in the city's ethnic composition was emphasised in the media, some migration has displayed continuity with past migration pattwerns. For example, there were strong recruitment drives in Scotland and Ireland. In 2013, the most common birthplaces for those working in the construction industry in greater Christchurch were New Zealand, 81.1 per cent; United Kingdom and Ireland, 9.4 per cent; and Asia (including India), 2.4 per cent. At the 2013 census, of the overseas-born people living in greater Christchurch who had arrived in New Zealand since the 2010–11 earthquakes and stated the industry they worked in, around half of those born in Ireland (51.5 per cent) and Brazil (47.8 per cent) were working in construction. Around a quarter of those born in England (22.4 per cent), the Philippines (24.5 per cent) and Scotland (29.3 per cent) were working in construction.[7]

Alongside the recruitment from the British Isles, employers looked to fill jobs from the supply of cheap labour available in a global marketplace, creating the potential to change the composition of Christchurch's ethnic make-up. In 2013, the Canterbury Employers' Chamber of Commerce settlement support coordinator, Lana Hart, reported that Filipino workers had recently outstripped British and Irish workers as the city's main source of new migrant labour. In 2013 New Zealand construction company Arrow International signed a deal with the China State Construction Engineering Corporation (CSCEC). The plan was for CSCEC to supply steel and workers for major building projects on which Arrow might bid.[8]

With the new migrant workers came concerns over working conditions. 'Do we have slavery in New Zealand?' Belinda Bonzon-Liu asked in August 2014 when speaking about the rebuild and conditions faced by Filipino migrant workers. Bonzon-Liu believed that some workers were paying recruitment fees of up to $20,000 and were fearful of deportation if they complained to employers, while others were trapped by substandard work and terrible living conditions and faced mounting debt, all of which were characteristics of bonded labourers.[9]

These post-quake migration patterns rupture Christchurch's ethnic past and promise a newly cosmopolitan city. The dominant stories told about Christchurch's history have emphasised class and ethnic isolation, and concentrated on the culture of Anglo-Celtic settlers. For example, Gwenda Turner's 1999 book, *Christchurch: An Enchanted Journey through the Garden City*, intended for general readers, starts with four ships bringing the 'first settlers to Christchurch'.[10] The focus is on colonial architecture and a garden city, and there is no mention of Ngāi Tahu as first peoples before European settlement, despite the 1998 Ngāi Tahu Crown Settlement Act. This is a Pākehā-centred view, involving the development of an identity that disregards Māori, let alone any other ethnicities. A slightly earlier example is the discussion that took place in May 1973 about placing a Māori symbol at the centre of the city in Cathedral Square. Megan Woods writes: 'There was, however, official resistance to such an overt inscription of Maoriness onto the landscape of the city with the reputation of being the most "English" of New Zealand cities.' Instead, in 1974 local architect and chair of the Council's Advisory Committee on the Urban Environment, Peter Beaven, suggested that a fountain that added a 'Mediterranean feel' would be more appropriate. The committee also considered 'trees and shrubs arranged with seats and tables' for the site.[11]

Following the 'Ngai Tahu Battles', fuelled by European colonisers who assisted with muskets and transportation, Māori living in the region were 'altogether at a low ebb on the eve of European occupation of their ancestral lands'.[12] As Te Maire Tau writes, from the late 1820s to the mid-1830s, Ngāti Toa, under the leadership of Te Rauparaha, 'seriously threatened' Ngāi Tahu's tribal domain.

‘Embroiled in conflict’, Ngāi Tahu suffered significant and traumatic losses.[13] The battles were fought on a scale that cultural encounter between Māori and Pākehā inherently influenced. Peace was made between Ngāi Tahu and Ngāti Toa only in 1839, a year before the signing of the Treaty of Waitangi.[14] Te Rauparaha released Ngāi Tahu captives on the eve of New Zealand becoming a British colony.[15]

European settler narratives were written onto this space. The first settlers were keen to farm the plains. In 1843, brothers William and John Deans came to Canterbury from Scotland via the Wellington region and attempted to settle on land at the place they called Riccarton. Although initially refused even a squatting licence by the government authorities,[16] eventually the Deans brothers were given permission to squat – so long as it was not on Māori-owned or cultivated land.[17] Their first cottage on the site was claimed to be the oldest building on the Canterbury plains – at once negating prior structures of Māori settlement.

In 1852, John Deans returned to Scotland to collect his bride Jane. Their son John was born in August 1853. Despite setbacks, in particular the deaths of William in 1851 and John in 1854, the family became important in the province, establishing an inland property at Homebush. Jane remained at Riccarton after her husband’s death, overseeing the family properties until her son John came of age in 1874, and hosting visiting dignitaries for many years. In 1914 the family gifted its remaining property at Riccarton to the city. The Homebush homestead was dramatically ruined in the 4 September 2010 earthquake.[18] Prominent descendants include rugby player and coach Robbie Deans, singer Julia Deans and artist Austin Deans.

Between 1844 and 1863, the Crown bought Ngāi Tahu lands in a series of nine purchases. The largest of these was the Canterbury Purchase of 1848, in which twenty million acres were bought for £2,000. As Atholl Anderson and Te Maire Tau write, 'Thus, in the space of only one generation, Ngai Tahu chiefs signed away, to the legal satisfaction of Crown agents at least, nearly 999 acres out of every 1,000 they had owned, and the great migration of Pakeha began.'[19] As Geoffrey Rice has put it, 'the process was neither straightforward nor fair'.[20] And Vincent O'Malley suggests that the low payment and 'miserly' allocation of ten acres of reserves per person were sweetened by promises of schools, hospitals, roads, welfare and general protection.[21] At a time of rapid change, confusion and mistakes could easily happen. For example, surveyor Charles Torlesse wrote in his diary on 12 September 1849 that he was 'Exploring Kiapoi: but could not ascertain the boundaries of the native reserve as the men were all absent.'[22]

There was cultural misunderstanding over what land and resources would be retained by Māori. For example, Ngāi Tahu did not believe that they had sold the inland districts, and thought that large reserves would be surveyed, that food-gathering areas would be set aside, and that there would be schools and hospitals within their villages.[23] Unsurprisingly, they soon attempted to get redress for the loss of their land. There were on-going petitions to Queen Victoria, to the New Zealand Parliament, to the 1868 sitting of the Native Land Court, and to the 1879 Royal Commission on land sales.[24] With important implications for Ngāi Tahu's place in the city, Chief Judge F. D. Fenton of the Native Land Court declined the iwi's applications for reserves within Christchurch boundaries in 1868 on the grounds they did not conform to Pākehā rules of producing plans and survey maps as proof of occupancy. The areas claimed by Ngāi Tahu were Otautahi (near the Kilmore Street fire station), Puari (where the High Court is), Taitapu Otokitoki (Lyttelton Harbour), Te Oranga (Horseshoe Lake), South Brighton Spit (the Estuary), Rapaki, Sumner and Bromley.[25] That is, Ngāi Tahu settlements and valued hunting and food gathering places were spread throughout the area that became Christchurch.

In his history of the Deans family, Gordon Ogilvie captures the importance of interaction between Māori and colonisers in the 1840s, and describes the significance of Riccarton to both. Part of Ngāi Tūahuriri territory, it was a valued mahinga kai (food gathering) place. William and John Deans 'demonstrated successfully that the plains and inland foothills were suitable for agriculture and stock breeding, that settlers could fashion a living there and that peaceful co-existence with the few surviving Maori was feasible'.[26] In June 1843 at Wairau, fighting broke out between Europeans led by Captain Arthur Wakefield, and the Ngāti Toa chiefs Te Rangihaeata and Te Rauparaha who opposed the methods of land purchase in the area. Twenty-two Europeans and four Māori died, and the consequences for race relations in the South Island were significant. Colin Amodeo ponders whether the incident served to ease the way for the Deans, suggesting that Ngāi Tahu were keen to maintain a good relationship with the Europeans and to avoid conflict.[27]

The forested area on the Canterbury Plains that was renamed 'Deans Bush' was known to Ngāi Tahu as Putaringamotu, 'the place of an echo'. Ogilvie portrays Putaringamotu as a Garden of Eden-like paradise:

> once a green haven of bush, flax and river in a sea of tawny tussock ... it was utopia, a site resplendent with eels, native trout, flounders, freshwater crayfish, whitebait and lampreys in the river. Kaka and kereru

in the forest. Weka and native quail in the grasslands. Grey and paradise duck in the swamplands nearby.[28]

The Deans were successful in large part because they understood that they needed to develop a good relationship with Māori. Ogilvie writes:

> William got on well with the Maori he met. He admired their religious fervour and their practical skills. He had experience from his time at Port Nicholson, prior to coming to the South Island, where he had learned to barter with Maori, and to speak the language.[29]

Securing a right to the land required careful negotiation amidst ongoing difficulties, including an 1845 earthquake.[30]

It was as a result of the good relationship between Māori and Pākehā that Ngāti Tūahuriri chief Te One Te Uki, who was in charge of Putaringamotu, appealed to Superintendent Richmond in Wellington for the Deans, still squatting on the land, to be allowed a lease.[31] In August 1845, the government consented. Another year passed before the Deans signed a lease agreement with Te Uki and his fellow chiefs in December 1846. There were fourteen Māori signatories. Harry Evison considered the lease 'a notable bargain for the Deans'. For £8 a year, they secured grazing rights to land covering approximately 29,000 hectares for twenty-one years. Although it was a small payment, following correct and formal Māori protocol was of immense value.[32]

Deans family recollections of the first years at Riccarton suggest they remained on good terms with Māori. There were reports in culturally unaware newspapers of the Deans being molested by Māori and having a stockyard destroyed, but this was untrue. In fact, a minor chief had merely threatened to pull down the yard as an act of utu (revenge).[33] At this time, cultural contact was lively and pervasive. A rare mention of Māori by Jane Deans hints at the vital, yet largely assumed, part they played in the early years of settlement. She writes:

> I have mentioned before that the Maoris used to plant and dig the potatoes in the fields for many years. A few months before the house was finished, but after it was roofed, they set fire to their huts (then on the island) in the hope that they would be allowed to occupy the new house. I stood firm in resisting their petition to do so, but allowed them use of the 'old barn' till they erected other huts down the riverbank near the railway bridge.[34]

Reflecting on the lease to the Deans, Tipene O'Regan argues that Ngāi Tahu had become familiar with sheep and cattle, and 'had a shrewd awareness of prices and product opportunities. We were ready to share our land and apply our new skills.'[35]

Such interactive beginnings where, on balance, the arriving settlers were dependent upon Māori, were soon forgotten. Matriarch Jane Deans went on to become the embodiment of a 'Canterbury pilgrim' and a member of Christchurch's élite – though she was both 'pre-Adamite' (having arrived before the 'first' ships), and a Presbyterian Scot in a Church of England settlement. She took it upon herself to create and add to the mythology of the 'pilgrim settlers' and in her twilight years wrote letters to her grandchildren, reinforcing beliefs about the Deans dynasty. There is little mention of Māori or of the formative experiences of cultural encounter in these letters. On the contrary, she wrote: 'When you grow older you will hear all about the Pilgrim Settlers, otherwise what I want to tell you is about the place they came to, a desert wilderness.'[36] Such sentiments fit with Vincent O'Malley's contention that the South Island was 'terra nullius' to arriving Europeans.[37] Influenced by a sense of advancing progress and civilisation, Jane Deans recounted seeing Christchurch for the first time in 1852. She remembered it consisting of swampy fields on each side of the road, 'almost impassable' and 'covered with tall flax'. The Deans buildings were 'the only signs of civilization' visible to the pilgrims.[38] The plains in their 'original state' were, to her, wild and untamed, waiting for 'a white race of people to reclaim them and make them useful or beautiful as a garden'.[39] Here the intention to civilise and cultivate is very clear. Jane Deans was looking back on a city that had become a self-conscious model of colonial practice. The cultural interaction so essential for settlement had disappeared, replaced by Christchurch as a blank slate to be filled in by Pākehā.

Another dominant settler story is that of Christchurch's *Mayflowers*, the 'first four ships'. The *Charlotte Jane, Randolph, Sir George Seymour* and *Cressy* set sail from Gravesend in September 1850 with more than 700 men, women and children. They arrived in Lyttelton from mid- to late December 1850.[40] Those on board came to be known as 'pilgrims' to a new land. Like newcomers elsewhere, they went on a rite-of-passage journey – in this case, up the Port Hills to gaze on the Canterbury Plains, and then down to makeshift accommodation. These first ships acquired almost mythical status in the Canterbury settlement, with descendants of their passengers claiming social superiority over those who followed. In reality there was little to distinguish these from later ships, including the *Castle Eden* and *Isabella Hercus*, that arrived in the first four months of the Canterbury settlement, bringing 1,293 settlers to Canterbury.[41] The myth that they found a terra nullius on arrival has likewise persisted. In 2000, Governor-General Sir Michael Hardie Boys commented that those ‘pioneers’ on the ships were ‘hardworking, practical people – a mix of builders, traders, craftsmen, professionals, workers, farmers – who established for all who came after them a way of life ... They found swampland, and bequeathed a city.’[42]

It wasn’t just Ngāi Tahu and the Deans family who lived in Canterbury before the first four ships. Colin Amodeo has drawn attention to the ‘forgotten forty-niners’, those Europeans and Māori who did the essential work necessary to pave the way for the first shiploads of Canterbury Association settlers. As further evidence of the essential support of Māori in early colonising endeavours, at least 120 skilled Māori from the Wellington district were hired to build the road from Lyttelton to Sumner.[43] Amodeo points to the irony of bringing recent enemies of Ngāi Tahu back to the South Island, but as they were peaceful Christian converts, according to Godley, all was well.[44] From September to November 1849, they were joined in their labours by Ngāi Tahu from Rapaki and other villages.[45]

As the new city grew, the interaction between Māori and Pākehā for trade and labour continued. Christchurch’s market square, later renamed Victoria Square, became a central contact zone. Geoffrey Rice writes: ‘There is some evidence that local Maori made full use of the Market Place in the early 1850s, selling potatoes and other produce to the early settlers of central Christchurch.

Presumably the produce was grown at Kaiapoi or Tuahiwi and brought to town on horseback.'[46] There was a lively trading environment, with dogs and horses 'allowed to roam freely while produce and money changed hands'.[47] But the initial dependence of the new settlers upon Māori soon declined. Atholl Anderson argues that over the course of the 1850s Ngāi Tahu settlement became confined to the reserves, and European immigration operated on a large scale, resulting a decline in all forms of trade and exchange between Ngāi Tahu communities and settlers. In Christchurch especially there was some trade in firewood from the reserved Ngāi Tahu forests, but Māori were progressively denied access to many of their former sources of commodities and could produce very little from their subsistence farms and fisheries.[48] Initial shared access, along the lines Ngāi Tahu had probably envisaged, came to an end from the 1860s as Māori people were progressively pushed to the margins.

More than other parts of the city, Victoria Square continued to have a changing and sometimes tenuous Māori presence. Over 300 Māori from around Canterbury took part in the Queen's 1887 Jubilee celebrations.[49] The statue of Queen Victoria, still standing in that square, has four bas-reliefs that hint at the cross-cultural interaction that was an essential part of the past. One depicts the arrival of the Canterbury pilgrims in 1850, and another their welcome by local Māori. It took until 1994 for a Māori monument to appear in Victoria Square to 'complement' the statues of Queen Victoria and Captain Cook. Riki Manuel's pou was carved from West Coast tōtara and told the story of the peoples who occupied the land prior to European settlement. Not everyone welcomed its presence: vandals tried to set it on fire twice in 1995. At the time, Manuel thought that the attacks might have been a reaction to the attacks on Pākehā monuments at Whanganui's Moutoa Gardens.[50] In post-quake Christchurch there is controversy over new plans for Victoria Square, with some wanting it kept similar to the way it was pre-quakes and others seeking a new look. The 2015 council decision to restore the Christchurch Town Hall, located at the edge of the square, tips the balance towards a conservative outcome which favours restoring wthe past rather than forging a new future. Symbolic of a tentative Māori presence, the pou is currently removed due to renovations in the area where it stood.

It can be argued that because of land loss, and a concentration of population outside of the city, Ngāi Tahu remained largely separate from city life until the 1930s. Even a model pā included at the 1906–07 Christchurch International Exhibition was established mainly with the assistance of North Island Māori. During the inter-war period, Ngāi

Tahu started performing and appearing during royal visits. Leaders such as Hoani Maaka and Christ's College-educated Te Aritaua Pitama, influential in regenerating Ngai Tahu's cultural identity and keeping alive the case for compensation, emerged. After the Second World War, increasing numbers of Ngāi Tahu began to leave their villages that 'ringed the city' – Tuahiwi, Taumutu, Rapaki, Onuku, Wairewa, and Koukourarata – and move to Christchurch in search of employment.[51] This can be seen as part of a broader pattern in which Christchurch has been the site of a continual series of labour migrations, including after the earthquakes.

As Megan Woods has written, from 1954 the Methodist Central Mission, members of Ngāi Tahu and the Department of Maori Affairs began to actively encourage young North Island Māori men, particularly from the East Coast, to move to Christchurch. In a scheme that lasted three decades, prefiguring post-quake migration patterns, thousands of young North Island men came to Christchurch to learn a trade. Many elected to settle in the city after completion of their apprenticeships.[52] The Department of Maori Affairs trade training schemes offered carpentry, painting, decorating and panel beating apprenticeships. There was also seasonal work at freezing works and the Kaiapoi Woollen Mills.

Angela Wanhalla has noted that 'sustained and extensive interracial marriage is often invoked in the southern regions, and is what distinguishes Ngāi Tahu from the trajectory of culture contact experienced by northern tribes'.[53] Historically, this high level of intermarriage, along with Ngāi Tahu's perceived loyalty to the Crown, led to a widespread perception of South Island Māori as being more assimilated than their North Island counterparts. Writing in the 1940 national centenary publication *The Maori People Today*, Roger Duff of Canterbury Museum described Māori people in the South Island who through generations of intermarriage and miscegenation were 'Polynesian in appearance' and 'European in work habits'.[54] Following the war, and in a climate of integration, many within the Department of Maori Affairs thought South Island Māori modelled the ideal citizenship that they wished to instil in Māori throughout the country.

In the post-war period, the Māori portion of the population of Christchurch soared. The 1945 census showed a Māori population of only 589, or 0.4 per cent of the population. By the 1976 census, Christchurch had a Māori population of 6,579, or 2.3 per cent of its population – a tenfold increase. Indexed to its 1945 population, Christchurch's rate of urbanisation was on par with the North Island cities of Wellington and Auckland, and Megan Woods argues that from 1966 Christchurch actually had a higher rate of urbanisation than the often-examined Auckland, although, of course, the numbers involved were lower.[55]

Migration changed Māori political dynamics in Christchurch. As the tribe holding mana whenua (authority over the land), Ngāi Tahu found its distinct status at risk of being overlooked with the arrival of new Māori in the city. For example, Ngā Hau e Whā marae on Pages Road, opened in 1990, was originally proposed in the 1850s as a place to rest for Ngāi Tahu moving from Banks Peninsula to Kaiapoi and for those working in the Christchurch markets. In the post-war years it was advocated as a sort of 'public community centre', a space shared between Ngāi Tahu and 'other Māori' – to the chagrin of those who valued continued recognition of tribal distinctions. Ngāi Tahu had wanted a space at Hagley Park, located in the centre of the city rather than on the outskirts, but this did not eventuate.[56] In 1960 Rēhua marae, a collaboration between the Methodist Church and the Couch family of Rapaki, opened in Christchurch city just outside of the central four avenues.[57] It became the site of the Maori Trade Training Scheme, where North Island Māori were welcomed to Christchurch by Ngāi Tahu.

Despite entrenched attitudes that led to invisibility and marginalisation, in the post-war years Ngāi Tahu underwent a renaissance, to become a major economic player. Attempts to redress past land loss had begun much earlier: in 1920, the Chief Judge of the Native Land Court recommended that £354,000 be offered to the iwi, and in 1944 the Ngai Tahu Claim Settlement Act provided £10,000 annually for 30 years and set up the Ngai Tahu Trust Board to administer the claims.[58] In 1986, Ngāi Tahu went to the Waitangi Tribunal, whose report was published in 1991. In 1992 there was a fisheries settlement, and in 1995 an ancillary claims settlement. Then the 1996 Te Runanga o Ngai Tahu Act created the tribe as a political entity. The process culminated in 1998 with the ground-breaking Ngāi Tahu Settlement Act, which provided $170 million in returned land and cash, plus the right to buy certain Crown assets, and a built in 'relativity clause' if other tribes were awarded more in their claims.[59] Those supporting the status quo for Christchurch were unsure of the implications of Ngāi Tahu's Treaty settlement, and there was some alarmism.

In the years since, Ngāi Tahu has established itself as a powerful, modern economic player with influential business interests in property, tourism and fisheries.[60] Ngāi Tahu Holdings Corporation was formed as the iwi's commercial arm, and Ngāi Tahu Property Limited developed assets with a market value in excess of $550 million. Around the time of the earthquakes, Ngāi Tahu had developed an investment portfolio of prime Christchurch properties, including the Christchurch Courts Complex, Armstrong Prestige in Moorhouse Avenue, the National Trade Academy, Turners Car Auctions, Tower Junction Megacentre Bulk Retail Centre, Tumara Park, Wigram Village (discussed in Chapter 5), Sockburn Business Park and the former Addington Prison site (discussed in Chapter 4).

By the twenty-first century, the status of Ngāi Tahu had dramatically changed. One potent example of this is the Christchurch Civic Building/ Te Hononga. Where once Ngāi Tahu had operated largely outside of city boundaries, a public–private partnership between Ngāi Tahu Property and the Christchurch City Council placed it symbolically at the centre of the city's governance.[61] Under the direction of architect Ian Athfield, the former New Zealand Post building was converted into New Zealand's first office building with a sustainability rating of six green stars, and opened in 2010. It was damaged in the earthquakes, but has re-emerged as a strong symbol and hub for the post-quake city.

Post-quake partnerships and enterprises represent an extended collaboration between Ngāi Tahu and Pākehā, in which everyone has changed. The hope for overcoming ethnic isolation is stronger than ever, and the possibilities for collaboration and mutual benefit are to the fore. Atholl Anderson and Te Maire Tau point out that both Māori and Pākehā have undergone much change since the early 1800s. They conclude that '[t]he histories of Maori and Pakeha New Zealanders are not so radically different' and that 'genetically and culturally there is very little difference between the descendants of the early European settlers and modern Ngai Tahu'. Both Māori and Pākehā 'have a story that tells of a people who crossed the oceans to a new country, and who became Tangata Whenua – people of the land'.[62] Their bicultural framework leaves the place of other ethnicities in question.

With the rupture of the city, an opportunity emerged for further rethinking of the past and planning for the future. In particular, there is a call for Māori to be officially and fundamentally involved in the rebuilding of the city. For example, the Te Rūnanga o Ngāi Tahu (TRoNT) submission concerning the draft of the Central City Plan stated that there were 48,000 members of Ngāi Tahu on the tribal roll, 7,000 of them in in Christchurch. TRoNT now has a 'special working relationship' with other city authorities, and has a wide range of concerns including culture and language revitalisation, environmental management, regional economic development, leadership development, education, and direct distribution of tribal funds. Capturing the extent of the historical shift in perspective, Maruhaeremuri Stirling of Ngāti Tūahuriri and Ngāi Tahu commented in a submission on the draft

Central City Plan: 'When I walk through the city I wish to see my Ngāi Tahu heritage reflected in the landscape. Our special indigenous plants that we used for scents, weaving, food and medicine are something unique that we can all celebrate.'[63] At the moment of rupture aspirations for the future are running high.

The Canterbury earthquakes have also set in motion a new wave of Māori migration to the city. Simon Lambert's research has shown that many of these recent arrivals are from the North Island, and like the international migrants, they have moved to Canterbury to find 'rebuild/recovery' work.[64] The proportion of Māori living in greater Christchurch increased 12.4 per cent between 2006 and 2013, when the Māori population reached 34,371. This was a bigger percentage increase for Māori than in Wellington or Auckland over the same period.[65] Māori unemployment was high in Christchurch before the earthquakes, and while some Māori on the unemployment benefit left after the quakes, the trend soon reversed. With shades of the past, the rebuild of the city is expected to offer long-term employment and trade training opportunities to Māori.[66] Evoking the Māori road builders of 1849 and the Māori post-war migration, the film *When a City Falls* includes footage of a Māori worker coming down from the North Island to help out through providing manual labour.[67]

Providing an indication of which Cantabrians were celebrated and placed on pedestals, just before the earthquakes local heroes from the second half of the twentieth century were publicly memorialised. The Local Heroes Trust commissioned twelve bronze busts by sculptor Mark Whyte. Members of the Trust included former Christchurch Art Gallery Trust chairman Chris Brocket, Arts Foundation New Zealand trustee Ros Burdon, Susan and Jim Wakefield, and architect Sir Miles Warren. The busts were placed on the edge of the Arts Centre on Worcester Boulevard. According to Ken Franklin, director of the Arts Centre, the aim was to recognise the 'endeavour and achievements' of 'fellow citizens', as 'champions' of 'the values that bind us'.[68] Sir Tipene O'Regan, who led the negotiation team for the Ngāi Tahu settlement, was the only Māori among the twelve 'heroes', described as 'Rakatira, kaumatua, writer, orator and teacher, principal negotiator of the Ngai Tahu Settlement, which brought many positive results for all of Canterbury'. The other selected heroes were drawn from the medical, commercial, philanthropic, arts, literary and sporting sectors. Frank Dickson, first chief executive of the Canterbury Savings Bank from 1962–1988, was chosen as a 'leader and inspirer of the team which created over $300 million of funds for the Canterbury Community'. Lady Diana Isaac, quarrying and construction company co-founder, was included for her work as a 'dedicated conservator of native birds, preserver of historic buildings', and for being 'a philanthropic benefactor to Christchurch'. Charles Luney, 'master builder of many of the foremost buildings of Christchurch, upright and respected contractor and employer for the 75 years of his working life', was commemorated. Sir Robertson (Bob) Stewart, 'businessman and industrialist, founder of PDL group of companies, pioneering exporter', was also positioned as a 'generous host and benefactor to many causes'. Likewise, Sir Angus Tait, 'father of the electronics and radio-communications industry in Christchurch, life-long supporter of research and development, generous benefactor of educational opportunities for others' was celebrated. Sir Don Beaven, 'Doctor, research specialist and teacher, loved and respected as the founder of diabetes research and care in New Zealand, tireless promoter of the healthy life' appeared.

The only sporting personality included was Sir Richard Hadlee, 'world class international cricketer, premier fast bowler and all-rounder'. His philanthropic efforts were also mentioned. After the earthquakes, and during the Cricket World Cup in 2015, his bust was moved to Hagley Park and a small shrine was created next to a walkway linking the cricket oval to the entertainment centre. Artist and teacher at Canterbury University

William Sutton featured, along with two prominent women writers. Elsie Locke, 'political, social and local community activist, well-loved historian and writer, determined and doughty fighter for the rights of the under-dog, active to the end', was there, as was Margaret Mahy, 'Christchurch children's librarian, world-famous writer of magical stories and verse for children and young adults, giver of the gift of imagination'. Both women are to be remembered in post-quake Christchurch through a new children's park on the former site of the Centennial Pool. 'Eminent architect' Sir Miles Warren, 'at the fore-front of building design for over 50 years, generous supporter of the arts and tireless worker for the betterment of Christchurch', and designer of the Christchurch Town Hall, was also in the line-up of busts. Warren has maintained a post-quake presence in the city, putting forward ideas for the rebuild.[69]

On the eve of the earthquakes Christchurch's local heroes were worthy candidates, but they did not reflect the true diversity of Christchurch. Important on a national and local level in the second half of the twentieth century were authors Keri Hulme, Alan Duff and Fiona Farrell, and television presenters Olly Ohlson, Danny Watson and Jason Gunn. Phyllis Guthardt and Jenny Harper were influential women in positions of leadership. A younger generation of heroes, largely but not exclusively emanating from popular culture, included Hayley Westenra, Bic Runga, Anika Moa and Eleanor Catton. The busts were already dated, and the city had become more multicultural, with a growing Pasifika population in particular. In the 1970s Sarona Meata'a Aiono-Iosefa, born in Christchurch in 1962, was from one of only two Samoan families at Burnside High School, the largest state secondary school in the country.[70] By the end of the twentieth century, a significant immigrant and second-generation Pacific Island community had added cultural diversity to Christchurch, leading to a flowering of 'decidedly *un*-English forms of art and expression'. A prominent example is the Pacific Underground of the 1990s.[71] It formed at the Christchurch Youth Centre and was a training ground for Dave Fane (actor, playwright and comedian), Oscar Kightley (actor, playwright and New Zealand Arts Foundation laureate) and Malo Luafutu (better known as Scribe).[72] Poet Tusiata Avia, whose book *Bloodclot* (2009) recast Nafanua, the Samoan goddess of war, as a young modern half-Samoan Cantabrian woman, is another Samoan artist born and raised in Christchurch.[73]

Racial tensions in the city in May 2004 signalled that increasing diversity was difficult for some. After a student from Vietnam was punched while walking in the street, an anti-racism rally was organised by Lincoln Tang and Hock Beng Lee. Comparing Christchurch to elsewhere, visiting Canadian academic Audrey Kobayashi wrote that 'The debate in all these cases, while ostensibly about migrants, is fundamentally about challenges to the dominant, long settled group and their established cultures of whiteness.' She also warned about 'the troubled space between an ideology of biculturalism and that of multiculturalism.'[74] Post-quake Christchurch poses an even bigger challenge for those antagonistic to the arrival of new migrants. In August 2015 Sake Aca, a migrant from Fiji, was subject to racist taunts by Lincoln University students while he played a game of club rugby. The incident led to extensive local and national media attention, feeding off the image of Christchurch as 'a monocultural place intolerant of ethnic diversity' and perhaps prompting 'a measure of soul-searching in Christchurch'.[75]

The earthquakes have brought race relations to the surface in Christchurch. A new wave of post-quake migration has led to further discussion about the ethnic composition of the city. Meanwhile, the dominant stories that have formed the city's collective memory are making room for Ngāi Tahu's rapidly changing post-settlement and post-quake position. There is an opportunity for reflection, dialogue and improvement. It is time to reflect upon the settler formation narratives of the Deans brothers and the first four ships, of cultural encounter in the nineteenth and twentieth centuries, and of Christchurch's local heroes on the brink of the earthquakes, to ponder past heritage and imagine a just and inclusive future that moves beyond solitude and separate identities.

3. HERITAGE

There is a belief among some of those living inside and outside of Christchurch that underneath the apparently conservative surface of the city there exists an ever-smouldering hotbed of radicalism. After the 4 September 2010 Canterbury earthquake, Auckland musician Don McGlashan captured the sentiment in an open letter of support for Cantabrians published in the *Press*, in which he referred to Christchurch as being like an old aunt who appears boring and ordinary, yet is really full of radical spirit, ideas and panache. The term 'radical' contains a number of meanings and strands, many of them complementary. In general, it refers to attempts to alter the dominant identity or status quo in society by political, economic, social and cultural means. From the late nineteenth century, Christchurch did indeed sustain an identity as a radical hotbed or stronghold.[1] New Zealand would be a different country without the city's radical streak.

This chapter reveals that until the Canterbury earthquakes, a placc with clearly defined and deliberate settlement, set on conserving its past, also had a heritage of radical people and ideas. Indeed, out of the potentially stuffy, backward-looking origin mythologies (discussed in Chapters 1 and 2) arose a place in reaction, spurred on by the constant threat of the conservatism at the city's bedrock. Following the ideas of Antonio Gramsci and Raymond Williams, the chapter argues that there is always an interactive relationship between dominant cultures and those who seek to challenge and change them. Such connection is an important feature of Christchurch's radical community, and the chapter demonstrates that Christchurch's radical and conservative heritages are not simple opposites. But what have the earthquakes done to Christchurch's radical past?

On the eve of the September 2010 earthquake, polls indicated that veteran left-wing MP Jim Anderton was set to win the Christchurch mayoralty in the upcoming October election. On 3 September he said that 'only an earthquake' would stop him. The quip was prophetic, and shortly afterwards voters overwhelmingly returned the incumbent, Bob

Parker. The earthquake had reverberations across the political as well as the physical landscape.

Prior to Parker's mayoralty, the city had been led by two left-wing, status quo-challenging mayors – Garry Moore and, before him, Vicki Buck, who in 2001 commented, 'I probably have a slight disregard or disrespect for traditional rules and for beliefs that are limiting.'[2] She had already come up against a barrier when she had been prevented from pursuing a PhD at the University of Canterbury part-time while she worked; she broke through a barrier when she successfully ran for mayor as an independent woman candidate who was pregnant.[3] It was during Vicki Buck's time as mayor in 1988 that Douglas Myers, former Business Roundtable head and beer baron, criticised the Christchurch City Council for its spending priorities and ideology of local government reform, describing the city as 'the People's Republic of Christchurch'. Myers's comment loudly backfired. He had inadvertently identified and rekindled an important part of Christchurch's identity – its radical political heritage. Buck was quick to capitalise on the situation, sending Myers a T-shirt labelled 'People's Republic of Christchurch'.[4] Car stickers emerged soon afterwards. She was able to tap into a radical political tradition in Christchurch that went right back to the time of settlement. It was a spirit of social capitalism or 'municipal socialism' involving the public ownership of public utilities and amenities for the benefit of all citizens.[5] Garry Moore continued this approach during his time as mayor, before the swing back to the right when Bob Parker took office in October 2007 championing the conservative spirit that also so clearly abounds in the city.

Many of the first colonists had a strong sense of the opportunity for reform. Among them was James Edward FitzGerald, the secretary of the Canterbury Association, who drafted the constitution of the Society of Canterbury Colonists and became the association's emigration agent. He arrived in New Zealand in 1850 and became the founding editor of the *Lyttelton Times*. He won the first election for superintendent of the province and later served as a member of Parliament.[6] FitzGerald was also a farmer. Edmund Bohan has argued that he brought a considerable Anglo-Irish influence to the colony.[7] David McIntyre has revealed FitzGerald's radical attitude towards race relations: he believed in equal civil and political rights for all New Zealanders. In particular, he advocated Māori political representation at all levels of governance, and suggested that the Māori King be made 'Superintendent of his own province'. He opposed land confiscation and colonisation by military settlers, and advocated the withdrawal of British troops.[8]

William Pember Reeves also looms large in Christchurch's radical history. Born in Lyttelton in 1857 to recently arrived British parents, Reeves was variously successful as a lawyer, politician, statesman, historian, poet, and long-term New Zealand Agent-General in London (he went cycling with George Bernard Shaw) and he became head of the London School of Economics in 1908. Remarkably for a Pākehā politician of the time, in 1895 he visited Parihaka to see Te Whiti.[9] Parihaka was a Māori settlement that under Te Whiti's leadership had become a centre for non-violent resistance to settler laws. On 5 November 1881 the government sent troops to sack the settlement. Te Whiti was arrested and served two years in prison, including Christchurch's Addington Prison, before returning to Parihaka. Reeves's visit to the Māori activist after his release was a radical act. He is more generally remembered as the 'rough architect' of the New Zealand state.[10] Historian Keith Sinclair considered Reeves to be more radical than any cabinet minister to come before him. He was particularly celebrated by the Labour Party when it came to power in 1935, and was admired by the party for introducing innovative labour legislation that most famously included the Industrial Conciliation and Arbitration Act 1894.[11]

Importantly, Reeves was a product of Christchurch. Jim McAloon writes that 1890s

Christchurch was 'William Pember Reeves's powerbase'.[12] Picking up on radical movements in Europe and the United States, he was influenced by American Edward Bellamy's 1887 utopian novel *Looking Backward* that in turn drew upon Henry George's *Progress and Poverty* (1879). Set in the year 2000, Bellamy's novel anticipated a range of innovations including global peace, land nationalisation, cooperative societies, piped music, reduced working hours, easy consumerism, shopping malls and credit cards.[13] Reeves wrote a series of essays based on Bellamy's ideas that appeared in his father's newspapers, the *Canterbury Times* and *Lyttelton Times*. Reeves's essays were also published under the pen name 'Pharos' in a booklet titled 'Some Historical Articles on Communism and Socialism'.[14]

Keith Sinclair highlights Reeves's upper class connections: he had grown up 'among the most prosperous, influential and educated people in Canterbury – and New Zealand'. His father William was elected to the House of Representatives in 1867, and Reeves went to the elite Christ's College and then on to study at Oxford University, returning to Christchurch to work as a journalist after he became sick.[15] The combination of 'gentry' background and social reformist beliefs encapsulates the bridge between conservative and radical in Christchurch, and was far from being an aberration in the city's history. It was a social combination that often, as in the case of William Pember Reeves and his wife Maud, or the Lovell-Smith family also discussed in this chapter, favoured Fabian socialism – that is, achieving socialism by democratic reforms rather than by revolution.

In the late nineteenth century radicalism's call for equality led to demands for women's rights. For women, to be radical meant to seek equality, independence and new opportunities. Christchurch was a hub for the hard work that it took to get the elected male politicians in Wellington to narrowly pass a Bill that allowed women to have a say in the governance of the nation, and that signalled the equality of women and men in society. Kate Sheppard, who spearheaded the national campaign for women's suffrage that resulted in New Zealand becoming the first country in the world to grant women the vote in 1893, did so from her Christchurch home. The achievement is celebrated in the women's suffrage memorial that stands in the city. As head of the Women's Christian Temperance Union franchise department, Sheppard led a non-violent, orderly and organised campaign of letter writing to newspapers and MPs; holding meetings, writing and distributing pamphlets, and keeping issues in the public eye. Importantly, mass petitions in 1888, 1891, 1892 and 1893 gathered signatures from women around the country. The last of these had a massive 31,782 signatures, representing one quarter of New Zealand's adult women.[16]

New Zealand lacked the obstacles that elsewhere impeded the progress of women's rights. In particular, it did not have a centuries-old entrenched conservatism, but rather was a place of rapid change and new ideas, and liked to consider itself 'God's own country' and a utopian paradise. Women's rights were part of a liberal progressive package of late nineteenth-century causes, and in Christchurch found an environment that fostered world-leading success.

Many local women seized the moment and had the resources necessary to agitate for the vote. Kate Sheppard reigns as the overall leader and there is no question that she was talented, dedicated and articulate. She was born Catherine Wilson Malcolm in Liverpool, England, in 1848, and raised and educated in Scotland. She migrated to Canterbury with other members of her family when she was twenty-one, following her sister Marie Beath who was already in Christchurch. Two years after her arrival, she married Walter Allen Sheppard, a storekeeper and Christchurch city councillor. Their only child Douglas was born nine years later. Sheppard outlived Douglas, who died in 1910; Walter, who died in 1915; and her only grandchild, Margaret Isobel Sheppard, who died in 1930. Aged seventy-seven years, in 1925 Kate married long-time friend William Sidney Lovell-Smith, another strong advocate for women's suffrage.[17] Lovell-Smith died four years later. Sheppard died on 13 July 1934, aged eighty-six, and is buried in the Addington Cemetery with her mother, a brother and a sister.

A key factor in the adoption of women's suffrage was the support of men in Parliament. Sheppard gained vital support from advocate Sir John Hall, the veteran conservative politician from Hororata, who was able to present the petition in Parliament. Jim Gardner considers that Hall 'may be reckoned the leading conservative politician in nineteenth century New Zealand'. He had moved to Canterbury in 1852 'drawn by the colony's pastoral prospects and Canterbury's Anglican ideals'.[18] The alliance between Sheppard and Hall is indicative of the bridge between radical and conservative at the time in Christchurch and in Canterbury more widely. Hall was 'establishment Canterbury' and hoped that votes for women would have the effect of promoting family values, settling wayward men and decreasing the problems caused by alcohol.[19] Suffragists and male politicians were united in their desire to tame wild frontier behaviour in a recently colonised land with a 'surplus' of men. Hence the moral and civilising value placed on women in the colonial context was at a premium. It was thought that votes for women would increase the influence of the family man against the 'loafing single man'.

Colonial feminists in Christchurch and further afield weren't solely concerned with suffrage but sought a wide range of changes, from legal improvements supporting women's equality to health and welfare reform. Sheppard unilaterally declared that 'All that separates, whether of race, class, creed, or sex, is inhuman, and must be overcome.'[20] She wrote widely on her beliefs about health and well-being, education, and social, political and economic justice. She considered alcohol and gambling to be evils ruining home and family, and advocated women's economic independence and equal pay for equal work. All these were concerns that have continued to resonate in radical Christchurch through to the present.

Symbolising and enabling new freedom, especially for young women, bicycles became rapidly available in the late nineteenth century. Zealandia Cycle Works in Christchurch manufactured machines that could be used as transport to and from school and work, or for recreation. Christchurch's flat terrain and temperate climate suited the bicycle, and the new invention enjoyed an extremely rapid uptake. As Clare Simpson writes, as a symbol of the 'new woman' the bicycle 'graphically represented a threat to the properties governing the behaviour and movements of respectable middle-class women in public'.[21] Cycling demanded new clothing, fostered sociability and brought women into public space in new, visible ways; bicycles were instrumental in challenging traditional roles.[22] Christchurch's innovative public health nurse, Nurse Sibylla Maude, rode a bicycle, as did some of her district nurses and radical health reformer Ettie Rout.

Christchurch had a strong 'radical dress movement' that advocated abandoning restrictive corsets and wearing divided skirts and bloomers to allow for greater movement – an important aspect of being a 'new woman'. In 1894 Kate Walker and J. R. Wilkinson married in a Christchurch 'Reform Dress Wedding'. Walker was clothed in blue knickerbockers and a long cream vest with gold embroidery, with a coat over the top. She wore a veil over her back rather than over her face and ditched the traditional orange blossom bouquet in favour of jasmine. In a photograph taken at the event, the bride towers over the groom and possessively places her arm on his shoulder. The Rational Dress Association had started in Christchurch a month earlier when Canterbury College refused to let student Alice Burn wear a divided skirt under her academic gown.[23]

There were, of course, many talented women leading the call for women's rights and freedoms outside of Canterbury. Amey Daldy, Meri Te Tai

Mangakahia, Harriet Morison, Mary Ann Muller, Helen Nicol, Annie Schnackenberg, Margaret Sievwright and Anna Stout were all prominent. But Christchurch is where the national suffrage effort was led, where radical dress reform was most prominent, and where a critical mass of feminists could provide impetus for other activities. For example, in 1892 the Canterbury Women's Institute was founded with Ada Wells as president; other members included Kate Sheppard, Maud Reeves, Eveline Cunnington and Edith Searle Grossman. This led to the establishment of the National Council of Women in 1896. Wilhelmina Sheriff Bain, who would go on to become an early peace activist, was treasurer.[24] Other Christchurch feminists at the time were Christina Henderson, Jessie Mackay and Sarah Page. Christina Henderson's sister Stella was one of the first women to study law, and her sister Elizabeth (McCombs) became New Zealand's first woman member of Parliament in 1933 – another first for Christchurch.[25]

Also contributing to a radical legacy that would last throughout the twentieth century was Helen Connon, a close friend of the feminist Edith Searle Grossman.[26] In 1881 Connon became the first woman in the British Empire to graduate with an honours degree. She is considered 'Canterbury's leading nineteenth-century woman academic and educationalist'.[27] Married to foundation professor

John Macmillan Brown, she had two children, Millicent and Viola, in whose lives Margaret Lovell-Smith writes, 'we see independence, courage and originality: surely an inheritance from their mother Helen Connon'.[28] Viola was an accomplished painter and part of Christchurch artists' association The Group until she went to Europe in 1935 to join Antonio Notariello, whom she married. Millicent married First World War conscientious objector Archibald Baxter, and their son James K. Baxter became a renowned poet and celebrated figurehead of the 1960s and 1970s counter-culture, involved in the alternative community at Hiruharama on the Whanganui River.[29] Throughout the twentieth century Christchurch would be home to a number of path-breaking academic women. Alice Candy taught History at Canterbury College in the first half of the century, and in the second half educationalist Jean Herbison and scholar, minister and university chancellor Phyllis Guthardt made it to the top of the New Zealand honours system, each being appointed Dame Commander of the Order of the British Empire.[30] Elsie Locke (see Chapter 2) made a sustained and important impact through her prolific historical and fiction writing. Women also played an important part in the Canterbury Workers' Educational Association, which was founded in 1915 to provide affordable and accessible adult education.[31]

Another important figure in the formation and cultivation of Christchurch's radical heritage was Professor Alexander Bickerton. Originally part of Canterbury's educational establishment, Bickerton was a chemist but taught all of the sciences as a foundation professor at Canterbury College in 1874. His radical beliefs and ways led to his controversial dismissal in 1902. Bill Metcalf suggests that with his bold lecture style, erratic dress, and belief in pacifism and communalism, Bickerton 'threated the staid conservatism of his peers'. His lectures included explosions, smells, magic and jokes.[32] An 1895 report of a special committee of enquiry into the Department of Chemistry and Physics (whose members included the Anglican Bishop of Christchurch) claimed to probe the management of the department: it reads as an inquisition. The report strongly implied that Bickerton was incompetent, lax, dirty and presiding over a declining number of students. It recommended '[t]hat Professor Bickerton be relieved of this subject, and that it be attached to the Department of Mathematics and Mathematical Physics, under the charge of Professor Cook' (Cook was another of the foundation professors).[33]

What did Bickerton stand for? He advocated flexible education, and considered his evening classes to be his most popular work.[34] He was also a strong advocate for women's education in the sciences, and was aware of the effort needed to encourage women to undertake scientific study, believing that girls struggled with 'the principles of inductive science'.[35] He commented: 'For some time I lectured to the Girls' High School, with the result that quite a number of the girls came to my classes, and now that I do not lecture scarcely any come at all'.[36] Bickerton had grand ideas for Canterbury, telling his inquisitors in 1895: 'Gentlemen – It possibly depends upon your report as to whether the higher education of the Colony remains the ridiculous farce it is at present or whether it becomes as vital, stimulating, and inductive as that of ancient Greece.'[37] Among his supporters were the generations of Canterbury students he influenced: mathematician John Angus Erskine, sexual health advocate and reformer Ettie Rout, architect and town planner Samuel Hurst Seager, left-wing member of Parliament for Sydenham Ted Howard, and nuclear physicist Ernest Rutherford are the most well-known.

Bickerton embraced a number of alternative beliefs popular in the late nineteenth and early twentieth centuries, including eugenics, socialism, anarchism and a new bohemianism that was critical of marriage.[38] Jim McAloon considers that 'Bickerton's views – decentralised, ethical and communitarian – could easily be described as anarchist'.[39] He wrote two utopian works:

Morganeering (1895) and *The Romance of the Earth* (1898), founded a community, and proposed many other projects designed to improve the lives of his contemporaries.[40] Bickerton was also another Christchurch radical who believed in bicycles. In 1901, when he was fined ten shillings for riding his bicycle on the footpath, he defended himself by arguing that the road was too muddy to ride on.[41] Such incidents revealed opposition to 'cyclists' rights' that continues through to the present. In June 2015, Alex Mann was convicted in the Christchurch District Court for 'impeding traffic' while biking on Dyers Pass Road in October 2014. He had not kept far enough left to allow traffic to pass him.[42]

From 1896 to 1903 Bickerton founded and played a large part in New Zealand's first intentional community. This was situated at a twelve hectare property on the edge of the Avon River, five kilometres east of the centre of the city. Bickerton named his home 'Wainoni', meaning 'curve in the water'.[43] A small lagoon on the property was turned into a lake.[44] The land was eventually used for low-cost housing in the 1960s as the city expanded eastwards to the sea, and has been significantly affected by lateral spreading as a result of the earthquakes. It is difficult to separate out the rumours from the reality of what happened at Wainoni's 'Federative Home'. Around thirty communards were in residence from 1896 until 1903. There were tennis courts, gardens, and many bicycles. Buildings included a billiard room, library, painting studio, photographic darkroom, workshop and conservatories. Some of the buildings were unusual, constructed cheaply but combining science and artistic creativity in their design.[45] As for the philosophy and everyday life at the commune, details remain obscure. Some members worked at the property and others worked elsewhere. All paid various amounts into the project. Despite Bickerton being against private property, 'he kept Wainoni in his own hands'. There were various attempts to manufacture and sell products, often inspired by Bickerton's science, such as the curative 'Wainoni remedy', medicinal soft drinks and fireworks. Domestic work was shared by the collective. There were rumours of 'free love', but married couples had their own private rooms.[46]

Expert on collective communities, William Metcalf, has reservations about the commune's success. He concludes: 'That Federative Home commune collapsed is no surprise. That it managed to start and carry on for five to six years is the real miracle.' This was because it 'had no constitution, a weak membership selection process, held all property in one name with most income earned by that person, a chasm of inequality, and no mechanism for conflict resolution'.[47] After Bickerton's dismissal from the university in 1902, the 'showman and entrepreneur' left the country, and until 1910 'Wainoni Park' operated as a pleasure garden for the amusement of the public.[48]

Exemplifying the Christchurch alliance of radical and conservative, in March 1908 at Wainoni there was a 'gathering of old colonists', those residents who were either born in the Canterbury settlement or who had arrived prior to 1870, and who shared the aim of setting up an Old Colonists Association for Canterbury. Surviving pilgrims from the first four ships met at a site strongly associated with radicalism.[49] Further ideological incongruence had occurred in 1895 when mock naval battles with strong military undertones were a part of the Wainoni fireworks celebration. And a few years later the muscular, conservatively Christian Boy Scouts found Wainoni Park a desirable place to camp.[50]

In August 1929 past differences were resolved when, following agitation from Ted Howard and others, Canterbury College rehabilitated Bickerton by appointing him Professor Emeritus. Only months later he was dead, assisted by ex-student and friend Ettie Rout, who gave him an injection of morphine and heroin and a bottle of whisky. His ashes were sent to Ted Howard and were interred in a column of the university's Great Hall

– demonstrating once more that establishment tradition and radicalism did co-exist.[51]

Despite the scepticism about the success of Bickerton's commune, many of the ideas it promoted were firmly embedded in Christchurch's radical imagination. The intentional community tradition lived on through the twentieth century and into the twenty-first. For example, the Chippenham Community was founded in 1971. Its location was a Benjamin Mountford-designed grand neo-Gothic brick house on Browns Road in St Albans, previously associated with the affluent Peacock, Brown and Acland families.[52] The commune grew quickly, adding a second house on adjoining Mansfield Avenue in 1972, and a forty-acre rural commune called 'Gricklegrass' near Oxford in 1973.[53] In 1996 the commune became the E Ngakau o te Takau Inc Heartwood Trust, and international experts on communal living have written of it as 'one of the most unusual collectives of intentional communities in the world'.[54] Future Labour Party MP Marion Hobbs lived there in the 1970s. It is still in existence as one of the oldest urban secular intentional communities in the world, although considerable earthquake damage has threatened its future. Funds are needed to restore the house, and there is talk of relocating it to Hagley Park.[55] Christchurch's communes had the ill fortune to be located in places heavily impacted by the earthquakes. The Creekside Community was a five-house complex on an acre of land occupied by a group of ten adults and eleven children in the 1970s.[56] It took its name from Dudley Creek, infamous after the earthquakes for extensive flooding.

Mentored by Bickerton, Ettie Rout personifies radical Christchurch, connecting the spirit of radicalism that flourished in the late nineteenth century to that which emerged and grew through the twentieth century. Rout supported many of the interrelated radical causes of her time: vegetarianism, rational dress to get women out of their corsets, the physical culture movement, votes for women, health and well-being reforms, and pro-labour advocacy. Rout was born in Tasmania, but it was the Christchurch context that made her, as it had done with fellow immigrant Kate Sheppard. The *Maoriland Worker* newspaper for which Rout worked for a time, editing six issues, in 1914 described Christchurch as the 'home of militant antimilitarism and socialist activity.'[57] During the First World War, the city's radical heritage influenced the formation of Ettie Rout's volunteer sisterhood of nurses. These women went to the war zone to nurse soldiers. Rout was determined to protect soldiers against venereal disease – a shocking intervention in the unmentionable area of men's sexual health.

Ettie Rout is often considered to have been 'ahead of her time'. Her writing during the 1920s on Māori culture, exercise and sexuality was considered by some at the time to be a hoax.[58] But as her biographer Jane Tolerton reveals, some of her ideas would eventually come to pass in the establishment of family planning clinics, women's health centres and sex counselling, the reform of divorce laws, state support for mothers and even the Māori renaissance. People would eat more soybeans, root vegetables and wholemeal. Debate at the onset of the AIDS pandemic in the 1980s echoed the politics of chastity versus 'safe sex' that concerned Rout during the First World War.[59] Naming Christchurch's AIDS clinic the Ettie Rout Sexual Health Clinic cemented the connection. But a few of her ideas were of their time. Perhaps the relative ethnic homogeneity of Christchurch and the colony's screening out of immigrants with poor health or disabilities led to the city also being a stronghold for eugenics. Rout's eugenic theories, influenced by Bickerton, are now dated and dangerous. Similarly, the otherwise progressive William Pember Reeves supported an Undesirable Immigrants Exclusion Bill in the 1890s. And less radical than Rout, but nonetheless concerned with health, eugenics, and fitness were Blanche Baughan, associated with the Canterbury Women's Club; and Cora Wilding, founder of the Sunshine

League and the New Zealand Youth Hostels Association.[60]

But not all health and fitness enthusiasts focused on eugenics. Harry Ell, a member of Parliament from 1899 to 1919, was a Christchurch radical and visionary who is remembered for his development of the Summit Road and its rest houses, and for advocating scenic reserves. The unemployed men who worked on the Summit Road during the Depression were known as 'Ell's Angels'. He was also concerned with social causes, supporting temperance and opposing gambling, and his maiden speech in Parliament foreshadowed outlawing the official use of the word 'imbecile'. Many years before, Ell had been a member of the Armed Constabulary in Taranaki, serving at Parihaka. He later recalled being ordered to uproot a Māori garden at Opunake, and reflected that such actions had 'brought about the bitterness and estrangement between the two races'.[61]

Peter Graham argues that until the late 1950s, Christchurch 'was New Zealand's cultural capital, a magnet for artists, poets, writers and musicians'.[62] Glynn Strange notes, for example, that under the direction of Professor James Shelley and then Dame Ngaio Marsh, the Little Theatre, home of the Canterbury University College Drama Society, from 1927 to 1953 'exerted an influence on New Zealand theatre far beyond its tiny dimensions'.[63]

The Canterbury College School of Art (now the School of Fine Arts at the University of Canterbury) produced a large number of successful painters including Viola Macmillan Brown, Ngaio Marsh, Evelyn Page, Rita Angus, Rata Lovell-Smith, Leo Bensemann and Olivia Spencer Bower. Rhona Haszard embraced the bohemian lifestyle of the 1920s, dressing eccentrically and advocating de facto relationships, vegetarianism and unprocessed food.[64] The radical strength of these artists flourished in opposition to the 'high arts' in the city, which Jonathan Mane-Wheoki has suggested was strongly English in origin. He argues that the amateur societies dominating the inter-war arts scene in Christchurch were 'culturally traditional, conservative, genteel, snobbish, stuffy and, above all, English'.[65]

With strong foundations in the nineteenth century, a Christchurch tendency to elect left-wing politicians enjoyed a long run until the Canterbury earthquakes. For example, in the first half of the twentieth century Tommy Taylor, Ted Howard and Harry Ell were prominent Christchurch MPs. The Sydenham seat as it existed between 1946 and 1996 was held by a succession of left-wing politicians: Mabel Howard (Labour) from 1946 to 1969, Norman Kirk (Labour) from 1969 to 1974, John Kirk (Labour) from 1974 to 1984, and Jim Anderton (representing in succession Labour, New Labour,

Alliance, and Progressive) from 1984 to 1996. In 1996 electoral boundaries were revised, with part of the former Sydenham electorate making up the seat of Wigram, which was held by Anderton from 1996 to 2011.[66] When Anderton decided to run for mayor of Christchurch instead of being an MP, Labour's Megan Woods won Wigram in 2011 and in the 2014 general election managed to increase her majority against the national trend.

Thomas (Tommy) Taylor was a Christian Socialist independent MP in late nineteenth- and early twentieth-century Christchurch. Taylor moved to Christchurch from Britain in 1874 aged twelve. Again, the local environment shaped him: Jim Anderton notes the 'radical intellectual culture' in Christchurch at the time, and cites the influence of F. J. Alley (father of Rewi Alley), Ettie Rout, Alexander Bickerton and cartoonist David Low.[67] Taylor went on to become only one of five members of Parliament to vote against New Zealand's participation in the South African War. When he died shortly after becoming mayor of Christchurch in 1911, more than 40,000 people turned out on the streets along the route to his funeral.[68]

A peak moment in the radical labour tradition occurred in 1972 when Norman Kirk became Prime Minister of New Zealand, a position he held until his death in 1974. Born in Waimate, Kirk had attended school in Christchurch. In 1953 at the age of thirty he became mayor of Kaiapoi, the youngest mayor in New Zealand. Kirk was the MP for Lyttelton from 1957 to 1969, when he transferred to the Sydenham seat.[69] His vision for the city and the region included supporting the construction of a road tunnel underneath the Port Hills to link Christchurch and Lyttelton and the development of a satellite town at Rolleston – a place that would experience rapid post-quake growth. In keeping with Christchurch's peace tradition, in 1972 Kirk withdrew New Zealand completely from involvement in the Vietnam War.[70]

Kirk was followed by new cohorts of Labour MPs, including locals David Caygill, Mary Batchelor and Ann Hercus. Jim McAloon has suggested that it was Christchurch's strong labour tradition that made its electorates desirable for leading Labour Party figures like Geoffrey Palmer, Jim Anderton, Mike Moore and Ruth Dyson.[71] In the 1990s and leading up to the Canterbury earthquakes this continued with politicians such as Lianne Dalziel, Tim Barnett, Brendan Burns, Megan Woods and Clayton Cosgrove. Representing the periphery, Christchurch-born Kerry Burke was MP for Rangiora from 1972 to 1975, then MP for the West Coast from 1978 to 1990. He served on the Canterbury Regional Council (Environment Canterbury) from 1998 to 2010, holding the chair from 2004. From the 1980s, however, some of

Canterbury's Labour MPs became followers of 'Rogernomics', advocating neo-liberalism and giving a new meaning to the term 'radical'.

On the eve of the Canterbury earthquakes, the majority of city parliamentary seats were held by the Labour Party. Then in the 2011 election, support for Christchurch-bred leader John Key's National Party in the seven Christchurch seats, including Waimakariri and Selwyn on the city's outskirts, jumped from 44.2 per cent at the previous election to 51.9 per cent – higher than in Auckland, Hamilton, Wellington or Dunedin. The nationwide swing to the right was driven by a massive 5.9 per cent swing in Christchurch. Labour managed to hang on to the electorate vote in Christchurch East, Port Hills and Wigram, but National's party vote was higher than Labour's in all of the city's seven seats. The left had ruptured.

In an article in the *New Zealand Herald* titled 'People's republic flies National's blue banner', Simon Collins wrote: 'The once-red "people's republic of Christchurch" has become the bluest of all the country's five main cities after a spectacular leap in support for the National Party following the city's devastating earthquakes.'[72] Particularly shattering for Labour was Brendan Burns's loss of the formerly safe seat of Christchurch Central. Popular ex-Canterbury Regional Councillor Nicky Wagner won the seat by only 47 votes.[73]

Had 'the People's Republic of Christchurch' ruptured once and for all? At the time, Labour's Christchurch East MP, Lianne Dalziel, said the change was in line with international experience that voters usually swing in behind incumbents after a disaster. 'There is a period of time within which the leaders at the time of the disaster enjoy popular support. Then, if things don't turn out well, they get blamed ... The next election will be completely different,' she said.[74] The local body election in 2013 was different, with Dalziel elected as mayor, but at the 2014 general election Christchurch stayed with the post-quake conservative status quo. Nicky Wagner retained Christchurch Central with a 2,168 majority over Labour candidate Tony Milne.[75]

As further evidence of a rupture in a radical socialist tradition following the earthquakes, at the beginning of 2015 the Christchurch City Council pondered whether it should sell its assets or keep on hiking rates as a means of dealing with an estimated $1.2 billion shortfall in funding. A brochure about a consultation document dealing with 'how we pay for our future over the next 10 years and beyond' included a letter from Mayor Lianne Dalziel and announced in large pink type that 'the earthquakes changed our city forever'. The full extent of the cost of repairing pipes, roads, services and community facilities remains unknown, and insurance proceeds and external funding amounts are uncertain. 'We can't just keep increasing rates and there are limits to how much we can borrow', the mayor stated – hence the suggestion of 'raising $750 million by selling shares in some or all of the Council's commercial companies wholly, or in part'. The Lyttelton Port Company is one such asset under consideration. The ruptured people's republic has been left 'trying to find the right balance between what we have to do and what we'd like to do', between 'fixing the city' and 'transforming it into a smart, green, liveable, sustainable, world-class city'.[76] Even the return as Deputy Mayor of Vicki Buck, formerly a strong advocate for social capital, is no guarantee that assets will not be sold.

The earthquakes have shaken up Christchurch's political landscape in multiple ways. For example, the campaign against the demolition of the Anglican cathedral has brought together a curious alliance across the political spectrum that would have been unthinkable in the pre-earthquake city. As discussed further in Chapter 5, ex-National Party MP, businessman and philanthropist Phillip Burdon and former left-wing MP and Deputy Prime Minister Jim Anderton have united as the Great Christchurch Buildings Trust to lobby for the restoration of the cathedral.

These contradictions are personified in 'The Wizard of New Zealand', widely regarded as Christchurch's Wizard. Ian Brackenbury Channell delivered lunchtime lectures outside the Christ Church Cathedral from 1974. He was closely aligned with Alf's Imperial Army, a 'pacifist warfare' group espousing antiquarian pro-everything-British sentiments. He refused to take part in the New Zealand census and painted Telecom's new blue phone boxes red in homage to the British Empire. As Geoffrey Rice prophetically wrote in 1999, 'It is now hard to imagine the city without his unpredictable presence'.[77] With his long hair and beard and his history of working as a university sociologist, he conjures up a combination of the alternative, anarchistic spirits of Professor Bickerton and James K. Baxter. Post-earthquakes, however, he has become a champion of the restoration of the cathedral that had long been the backdrop to his speeches.

Another important aspect of Christchurch's radical history has been its long association with the peace and environmental movements. The spirit of Wilhelmina Sherriff Bain, Kate Sheppard and others imbued the work of Elsie Locke, Owen Wilkes and Kate Dewes. As Maire Leadbeater, daughter of Elsie Locke and sister of former Green Party MP Keith Locke writes, in the second half of the twentieth century, peace and nuclear disarmament became part of New Zealand's radical psyche. Once again, Christchurch was a hotbed.[78]

In the 1960s and 1970s, a new generation

joined with the older in making a stand for nuclear disarmament and against New Zealand's participation in the Vietnam War. Norman Kirk's withdrawal of New Zealand troops from Vietnam provides a key example of inter-generational collaboration. But citizens' views could differ and there was a strong background of conservatism to overcome. On 11 November 1969, Remembrance Day commemorations were disrupted by the laying of wreaths to the dead and dying in Vietnam. The Progressive Youth Movement (PYM) in Christchurch laid a wreath inscribed 'to the victims of fascism in Vietnam'. As Elsie Locke writes, it was too much for the mayor, Ron Guthrey, who tore the wreath from the war memorial and flung it away. When people had moved on to a ceremony in the Anglican cathedral, the wreath was restored, whereupon the police removed it. Locke continues: 'A campaign for nuclear disarmament (CND) silent vigil for peace stood steadfastly by and maintained its dignity.' But the mayor had the ammunition he needed and proclaimed, 'Dumb, long-haired louts who have nothing to contribute to our society – who damn everything we have fought for – must not be allowed to insult our war dead.' On Anzac Day in 1971, the PYM carried a wreath for the Vietnamese and placed wooden crosses on the lawn beside the war memorial. The Returned Services' Association removed the crosses.[79]

Christchurch has also supported sustained protest against United States and New Zealand government facilities believed to be engaged in surveillance. In 1968, 4,000 people marched through Cathedral Square in the biggest anti-war demonstration the city had seen. It is estimated that 65 to 75 per cent of the student population took part, protesting against plans to build eight Polaris missile submarine navigation radio stations around the world, with one of them, a transmitter named Omega, to be constructed on the foothills of the Southern Alps. After eighteen months, Australia was chosen instead.[80] Norman Kirk, then Leader of the Opposition, also came out against Omega.[81]

During the 1970s, activist Owen Wilkes made connections between science and secret military pursuits at the United States Operation Deep Freeze Base at Harewood that was used for transportation to and from Antarctica. Christchurch-based Campaign Against Foreign Military Activities in New Zealand (CAFMANZ) protested at Harewood, arguing that the presence of the base made New Zealand a nuclear target.[82] By the twenty-first century the site continued but with a depoliticised presence. In an interesting post-quake twist, with so much of its own heritage destroyed, Christchurch has promoted its association with Antarctica and the base as part of the city's identity. Two 'Ice Fests' showcasing Christchurch as an

'Antarctic Gateway' have attempted to breathe new life into the city.[83]

Christchurch maintained its reputation as a stronghold for the peace movement in the 1980s and 1990s. Nationally and internationally significant peace activist Kate Dewes formed the Christchurch-based New Zealand Nuclear Free Zone Committee in October 1981. Dewes also instigated and organised the watershed visit of Australian physician and opponent of nuclear weapons Helen Caldicott to New Zealand in 1983.[84] From 1986 to 1996 she was instrumental in the internationally collaborative World Court Project that attempted to outlaw nuclear weapons.[85] Green MP Rod Donald also came to prominence in these decades. Educated at St Andrew's College, and often seen wearing a bow tie, he epitomised the connections between establishment and radical Christchurch. His green vision included promoting cycling and public transport and opposing the foreign economic control of New Zealand.

Christchurch in the 1980s also had vigorous feminist, anti-apartheid and other left-wing movements. The journal *Race, Gender, Class*, published in Christchurch, attracted contributions from around the country. The first editorial stated that the journal hoped to 'assist understanding and radical political action in the areas of Maori self-determination, feminism and socialism'.[86] Articles written in English included a Māori-language summary. Thirteen issues of the journal were published between 1985 and 1992. Contributors over the years included Vincent O'Malley, Tipene O'Regan, Jim McAloon, Belinda Trainor, Jane Kelsey and Steve Maharey.

Student involvement in protests from the 1960s through to the time of the earthquakes cemented their reputation as being lazy and oppositional, at least in the eyes of conservatives. On the eve of the Canterbury earthquakes, there was a new 'Roger's generation' of fee-paying students with drastically reduced entitlements. The emergence of the 'Student Volunteer Army' that assisted in the aftermath of earthquake damage gained widespread publicity, and even royal endorsement. The more silt students shovelled, the more their radical reputation liquefied. They were definitely in the city's good books, with claims that the work of the Student Volunteer Army had 'produced a lasting change in student attitudes and behaviour'. Riccarton Community Watch director Geoff Parfitt said students used to be the cause of most trouble in the area but now they were community-minded.[87] The ruptured radical reputation had its benefits. For example, the University of Canterbury was able to build a new student bar right on the campus boundary with Ilam School – a move hard to imagine elsewhere in the city, or indeed the country. Neighbourhood resident Andrew Gunn wrote in support of the bar: 'I won't forget in a hurry the sight of so many students from my neighbourhood trudging home tired and muddy after another day's shovelling in east Christchurch. Let them have their building – they deserve it.'[88]

There are signs, however, that a new radical wave for Christchurch will once again be led by newcomers drawn to the city by its radical past. 'Veteran protester' John Minto has moved from Auckland to Christchurch, and in mid-2015 he made his opposition to proposed council asset sales clear. Of Mayor Dalziel he said, 'I think she has sucked from the poisoned chalice of privatisation so often she is immune to its effects.'[89] Deputy Mayor Vicki Buck rallied to support the mayor.

The Canterbury earthquakes have ruptured the city's past and forced allegiances between radical and conservative. John Cookson has argued that a moderate streak has for long been a part of Christchurch.[90] In post-quake times, in some ways, it is now triumphing. It is unclear if Christchurch can look forward to a radical future that honours past tradition.

4. GOTHIC

While the first European pioneers were trying hard to create God's own country – a South Pacific garden paradise of enlightened minds – many of the shrines they built revived a Gothic architectural style. Neo-Gothic architecture, characterised by pointed arches, rib vaults, flying buttresses and large windows with elaborate ornamental stonework, was popular in Britain at the time Christchurch was colonised. The style was dramatic, drawing the eye sharply and clearly to the heavens, and proclaiming Christian civilisation and improvement.

The term 'Gothic' enjoys a variety of meanings, both scholarly and popular, that have endured or been adapted over time, depending on context. Gothic architecture, itself diverse, spanned the twelfth to sixteenth centuries; the neo-Gothic revival of the eighteenth and nineteenth centuries embraced not only architecture but also the heyday of the popular Gothic novel. This genre involved mystery and horror as themes, often in a pseudo-medieval setting. Examples of Gothic novels of the nineteenth century are Mary Shelley's *Frankenstein* (1818), Emily Bronte's *Wuthering Heights* (1847), Robert Louis Stevenson's *The Strange Case of Dr Jekyll and Mr Hyde* (1887), and Bram Stoker's *Dracula* (1897). Interest in romance, high emotion, mystery and horror was ideologically quite different from the utopian visions and 'garden city' and 'arts and crafts' movements that advocated bucolic living in harmony with nature, and that were also so popular later on in the nineteenth century. In Christchurch the neo-Gothic blended with other elements, including international trends and styles that were gloriously lumped together as 'Oriental'.[1] Other cultures were enthusiastically lapped up and adapted to the local conditions, with an important, dynamic and shape-shifting Gothic identity forming part of the city's character.

This chapter considers the ruptured Gothic. In his book *Plotting Gothic*, Stephen Murray argues that the Gothic phenomenon was not just a creation of masonry, wood and glass, but also a 'rhetorical construct'.[2] Likewise, this chapter explores the meaning of 'Gothic' in relation to Christchurch and its people. Christchurch's Gothic was supposed to be uplifting, morally positive and enlightened.

This 'good Gothic' involved promoting a dominant pan-Englishness. But this was not to be completely the case. A 'Christchurch Gothic' emerged that also involved a sinister and brooding sensibility. 'Dark Gothic' meant a threat to everything that Englishness entailed. In this chapter the good neo-Gothic of Eurocentrism and Englishness are juxtaposed with the darker Gothic narratives of the Parker–Hulme murder, and Addington Prison and Sunnyside Hospital. Christchurch's Gothic identity has constantly changed through time, by the end of the twentieth century culminating in aspects of heritage tourism. Since the earthquakes a post-apocalyptic landscape has emerged that challenges the 'English' and 'garden city' identities of the city. With the stage that framed the dark Gothic ruptured, there is a possibility to break from the Gothic past.

As Gothic sensibility is common in other British settler societies, Christchurch shares some similarities with the way it is manifested in other places. Australia's terrifying neo-Gothic penal buildings such as those in Tasmania, and Canada's authoritarian neo-Gothic structures such as Ottawa's Parliament Hill, served to subdue and control.[3] Christchurch's Gothic, however dark, somehow pales in comparison, and is softened by dreams of garden city living. Nonetheless, a Gothic quality has been repeatedly identified as 'an important aspect of national character', and it was particularly evident in pre-quake Christchurch.[4] Significantly, on board the *Charlotte Jane* in 1850 was Benjamin Mountfort, the architect who would play such an important role in creating Christchurch's, and New Zealand's, neo-Gothic character. Mountfort was responsible for the Provincial Council Chambers, Canterbury College, Canterbury Museum and Trinity Congregational Church, and he also helped to get the Anglican cathedral finished.[5]

One proponent of a 'Southern Gothic' located in Christchurch is cultural studies scholar Howard McNaughton. He points to the dark side of neo-Gothic architecture, exemplified by Addington Prison and 'Sunnyside Lunatic Asylum' (later known as Sunnyside Hospital). Sunnyside was the largest public building in nineteenth-century Christchurch and was designed by Benjamin Mountfort. McNaughton places both Addington Prison and Sunnyside in an 'abject zone'.[6] They represented the unsightly, fallen and desperate underbelly of the city. While its history fitted with an uneasy dark Gothic, Sunnyside combined neo-Gothic architecture with garden rehabilitative movements. Sunnyside was closed in 1999 and its demolition was completed in 2007. Then as part of the Ngāi Tahu Treaty Settlement, the site became a housing development.[7] There were mixed feelings concerning Sunnyside's demolition, ranging from arguments that it should be preserved and its history remembered, to the view that its demise was cathartic and a form of closure on difficult past events.

Meanwhile, Addington Prison, with its bleak rows of cells and its small windows, became 'wasteland, surplus to requirements and an embarrassing monument to an archaic penal system'. It was decommissioned in 1999 and Ngāi Tahu Property bought it. In 2002 it became a tourist site, and in 2003 student and backpackers' accommodation. McNaughton reads the prison landscape, noting its incarceration of Māori pacifist prophets Te Whiti and Tohu, who were at Addington in 1882. He juxtaposes and positions Christchurch as a place where 'the garden as an index of civility becomes a paradoxical veneer in the face of biculturalism and decolonization'.[8] While his focus is on the abject zone that appears in contrast to a 'good' Gothic, before Christchurch ruptured many of the 'good' Gothic revival buildings in the central city had also acquired a tourism purpose. That is to say, the contrast between 'good' and 'dark' Gothic was ripe for rupture. Indeed, by the time of the Canterbury earthquakes, the visible manifestations of the dark side of the Gothic were either demolished, such as Sunnyside Hospital and the Supreme

Court, or being used for tourism, as in the case of the former Addington Prison. And McNaughton's neo-Gothic precincts as sites of darkness and decay have nothing on the post-apocalyptic Christchurch landscape that has emerged.

As James Belich and Lydia Wevers noted, 'Many pundits have noted the strange dark side of Pakeha culture as a "New Zealand Gothic" reflecting a sinister side of Kiwi cultural identity, our innocence exposed.'[9] They argued, for example, that actor Sam Neill's 1995 documentary *Cinema of Unease* reviewed the New Zealand film industry by exploring themes of 'isolation, loneliness and the dark undercurrent beneath the seemingly uneventful surface of New Zealand life'; in other words, it was an articulation of a New Zealand Gothic.[10] Prominent in Neill's analysis was Peter Jackson's and Fran Walsh's 1994 film *Heavenly Creatures*, based on the 1954 murder of Honora Parker that has become an important part of Christchurch's and New Zealand's Gothic identity. In her analysis of *Cinema of Unease*, Brenda Allen points out that Neill was living in Christchurch (he attended Christ's College) at the time of the murder.[11] Amidst the glory days of post-war New Zealand lurked the strange, frightening and dark. The good Gothic and dark Gothic collided.

At the time, the murder sullied Christchurch's self-conscious identity as a respectable garden city, cutting to the heart of the Englishness so important in the construction of colonial Christchurch. Christchurch's garden city movement had its origins in the late nineteenth century. Samuel Hurst Seager, architect, town planner and conservationist, played an important role in developing the concept and reality, as did Leonard Cockayne, who established the garden competitions and fields of daffodils, and had an experimental garden at the upper Bexley Road near Wainoni. Harry Ell was also important in conservation, and with Cockayne saved Kennedys Bush.[12] At the end of the twentieth century, Mayor Garry Moore was still calling Christchurch 'the garden city', 'an international example of how an urban area can have forward-looking industry and superbly presented natural features'.[13]

Where to look to for expressions of that post-war garden city Englishness that along with the neo-Gothic has now ruptured? Beyond the written word, images can be incredibly evocative as texts, although the ways in which we read or interpret them are as complex and multifaceted as the ways in which we read written texts. Both film footage from particular time periods and historical recreations can allow the previously distinct categories of fact and fiction to blend into 'faction', in which creativity takes precedence over reality. As this chapter argues, this is especially the case when exploring Christchurch's Gothic identity. Crime, moral panic and the Englishness of Christchurch's social structure collided with neo-Gothic landscape.

One striking example of a film that might be seen as an historical source and that promotes a view of garden city Englishness is a 1952 Christchurch City Council film titled *Christchurch: The City on the Plains*. The film offers a hauntingly hegemonic narrative of clear-cut authority. Happy, uplifting music plays as the narrator introduces the city on a sunny spring day.[14] For the next eighteen minutes, the film showcases the major features of Christchurch's English identity.

What is really meant by 'Englishness', as a close viewing and interpretation of the film reveals, can more correctly be considered as a form of 'Britishness'. Scottish, and to a lesser extent, Welsh and Irish identities were broadly incorporated and conflated into a pan-Anglo-Celtic version of 'Englishness'. Such conflation is historically common and has actively served to promote assimilation to the dominant culture. Catherine Hall has argued that 'Englishness is not a fixed identity but a series of contesting identities, a terrain of struggle as to what it means to be English. Different groups competed for the domination of this space and the political and cultural power which followed from such domination.'[15] In Christchurch, an imperial Englishness, more homogeneous and confident than that found in Australia, Canada and the United States, was on display. This was possible because Christchurch's Anglican settlement served as a foundation for its English claims, just as Presbyterian settlement contributed to the enduring perception of Dunedin as 'Scottish'. As Marjory Harper writes:

From its conception by the Canterbury Association in 1848, Christchurch – through its very name and ethos, along with its carefully manicured gardens and some of its architecture – was to present the most visible face of an English identity that elsewhere in New Zealand, as in other parts of the British empire, was often obscured by more controversial or noisy ethnic groups.[16]

Christchurch: The City on the Plains describes the city as a Church of England settlement, but in 1952 its version of Englishness incorporates Roman Catholics and other denominations by showcasing the 'stately Cathedral of the Blessed Sacrament', as well as the Durham Street Methodist church and Presbyterian St Andrew's, 'the oldest wooden church in the city'.

Though situated in New Zealand, Christchurch was officially a Church of England settlement that was carefully and deliberately settled as a new part of the British Empire. As Chapter 2 has outlined, the story of the pilgrims on the first four ships formed a powerful foundational mythology. By

1880, roughly half of the population traced back to the pilgrims, after which the proportion was ever-declining.[17] The mythology, however, has clung on, even after the earthquakes, and has been revived and reinvented. American historian David Hackett Fischer, commenting on Christchurch's post-quake culture, quotes an unnamed journalist in the *New Zealand Herald* as saying that the spirit of the city is intact, by which is meant its English colonial origins.[18]

Probably because it was secure in its Anglican foundation, and because the proportion of Catholics was so low as to be 'unthreatening' to the dominant character, Christchurch was mostly able to incorporate Irish, Scottish and Welsh cultures into expressions of Englishness. As Lyndon Fraser has noted, few Irish-born Catholics ventured to the Province of Canterbury before 1859.[19] By the end of 1850, less than 3 per cent of the Canterbury population was Catholic. Then, from 1860, with the introduction of assisted passages for Irish Catholics, the numbers rose to make up 10.3 per cent of the population by 1878. This is not to say that ethnic and sectarian tensions were absent. For example, on Boxing Day 1879 there was a riot in which thirty Irish men with pick-axes attacked an Orange procession in Christchurch.[20] Stirring up versions of the past, in 1982 historian Stevan Eldred Grigg estimated that, by 1880, 20 per cent of foreign-born people in Canterbury were Irish, and that they had a reputation among the pilgrims for being dirty, drunken and Catholic.[21]

The 1952 film portrays Christchurch's physical environment as tame and beautiful. Hagley Park with spring daffodils in bloom is showcased, as are the 'garden suburbs' that make up the city. As John Cookson has argued, the city's location on a plain meant that it was geographically possible to tailor an English garden, and to keep indigenous features well out of sight.[22] This is emphasised through the film: Christchurch is described as a 'green and pleasant' land, a garden of Eden. Introduced deciduous flora enable greater recognition of distinct changes of the seasons, and willows remind citizens of 'how a river should look'. The film features the tree-lined Avon River as 'a small and placid stream' that is home to ducks and other introduced fauna. Even factories have gardens. Introduced cherry blossoms, azaleas and tulips are shown in bloom, the latter a nod to Dutch migrants. Dutch made up the biggest non-British migrant group during the post-war years: between July 1951 and June 1954 a peak intake of 10,583 Dutch settlers was recorded.[23] Tulips, with their Dutch associations, are brought under an English umbrella, just as Dutch migrants were welcomed to New Zealand because they were seen as compatible with existing populations and considered willing and able to assimilate into the dominant culture.

Parts of *Christchurch: The City on the Plains* display strong continuity with the hegemonic landscape markers analysed in Chapter 1. For example, Godley 'rightly' stands in the centre of the city and Captain Robert Falcon Scott is celebrated as a British hero. Other iconic structures mentioned include the Bridge of Remembrance that salutes New Zealand's war sacrifices for the British Empire. William Rolleston is acknowledged in stone outside of the Canterbury Museum, which is introduced as an 'arts and learning precinct' including the Canterbury University College, where Sir Ernest Rutherford studied and conducted early research, and the art gallery tucked away in the Botanic Gardens. The Provincial Council Chambers and the Christ Church Cathedral are also featured. Neo-Gothic architecture is characterised as 'English', pleasant and civilised.

It is said that in Christchurch the question 'Which school did you go to?' is an important form of class identification. The film features a number of Christchurch schools, emphasising the importance of education from kindergarten and primary school to high school and university. The state secondary schools, Christchurch Girls' and Boys' high schools, feature prominently, as does St Bede's Catholic school for boys with its 'green and pleasant grounds' and ivy-clad walls; the Presbyterian St Andrew's College with its pipe band; and the Anglican Christ's College with frost on its fields evoking the old world. Again, the impression is given of an 'Englishness' – one that is more properly considered 'Britishness' through its inclusion of all the nationalities of the British Isles. The newer co-educational state high schools that opened after this film was released remain largely outside of the 'old establishment' narrative.

Sport also plays a part in the promotion of Englishness. The film uses high school footage to identify health and fitness as an important aspect of living in Christchurch. The camera swoops from Christchurch Girls' High School, located in Cranmer Square, to the nearby Hagley Park with its playing fields for basketball (netball), hockey and rugby. Rugby is described as 'the national sport', with crowds gathering to watch the big games at Lancaster Park. Meanwhile, in summer at the 'woodland green' that is Hagley Oval, 'generations pay allegiance to the king of summer sports', cricket. In addition, there is rowing on the lower Avon, in a 'settling reminiscent of an English river'. Other English sports portrayed are archery, bowls, tennis, on 'the fine grass courts of Wilding Park' (named after Anthony Wilding, Christchurch's Wimbledon tennis champion who died serving in the First World War), and yachting at the Estuary which provides 'perfect sailing conditions for pottering about in small boats'. Surf lifesavers at New Brighton Beach hint at a wild environment beyond, but their orderly systems, epitomised in their drilling in straight lines, suggest that even the fearsome Pacific Ocean is under control.

Overall, the film promotes a very ordered and controlled environment. The emphasis is on regularity and a sense of calm. Even the 'heart of the city', Cathedral Square, is a 'quiet haven'. But the city is modern, too: buses, trams and cars travel along long, straight streets 'laid out in regular patterns by the pioneers, long ago'. In line with the emphasis on Christchurch as a healthy place, it is described as 'a city of cyclists', many of whose residents ride to school or work each day. Only Copenhagen is said to boast more bicycles. Extensive recreation and leisure activities available around the city and further afield are identified in the film, including those at Diamond Harbour and Governor's Bay, and the holiday cottages at Taylor's Mistake feature. Even Lake Pukaki and Lake Kaniere are included, and the film emphasises the wealth of the province generated through production of sheep meat and wool. The Canterbury Plains are introduced as 'the granary of New Zealand'. The Agricultural and Pastoral Show and trotting at Addington Raceway connect town and country.

Perhaps just as interesting as what is included

in the film is what is omitted. In a narrative of transplanted Englishness, indigenous people and indigenous flora and fauna are completely absent. The signature raging nor'west wind is left out of the picture. There are no overt signs that the film is about life in the South Pacific. There is no acknowledgement of the ways indigenous elements have been accommodated, for instance in exhibitions such as that of 1906-7, or in cultural adaptations such as Ettie Rout's physical exercise routines that took their name – waka – from the Māori word for canoe. Addington Prison and Sunnyside Hospital are definitely absent. Part fact, part fantasy, the film is important for the details it captures, and its confident assertion of picture-perfect Englishness. In post-quake Christchurch, there is nostalgia for such portrayals. People have coped with disaster by remaking the past. It was Christchurch of 2010 and 2011 that ruptured, but in the historical stories and images that have emerged, there is a sense of the years before being destroyed as well.

The 1994 film *Heavenly Creatures* begins with similar film footage to *Christchurch: The City on the Plains*, with a narrator introducing the picturesque and orderly city in which Pauline Parker and Juliet Hulme lived and went to school. The focus then quickly and starkly shifts to the macabre screaming following the 1954 murder of Honora Parker at Victoria Park in the Port Hills that overlook Christchurch. As James Bennett puts it:

> The travelogue sequences of mid-twentieth century Christchurch, provincial, orderly, white and conservative, are suddenly robbed of this bucolic veneer when juxtaposed with a hand-held camera following two blood-spattered girls running and screaming along a tunnel-like path. The underbelly of the city is suddenly exposed.[24]

Heavenly Creatures captures the intense fantasy worlds of the two teenagers, as gleaned from Pauline Parker's diary and brought to life by Peter Jackson's special effects. According to James Bennett, the film 'combines many genres and elements including surrealism, Gothic horror, black and white dream sequences, plasticine characters, introductory montage drawn from 1950s Christchurch commemorative documentaries…'.[25] Juliet Hulme's mother made sure that her daughter's diary was destroyed before it could be gathered for evidence – an act that obscured Juliet's motivations and allowed fictionalised accounts to fill the vacuum when explaining the tragedy.[26]

The film's juxtaposition of idyllic city and horrific murder suggests that there was something about the air-brushed image of Christchurch that was conducive to the rare and tragic matricide that took place – that is, that the good and dark Gothic identities of Christchurch were somehow interrelated. In a relatively small city, as Christchurch was in the 1950s, such an event was both sensational and deeply unsettling. Female murderers are rare, and females murdering their mothers even more so. In addition the young age of the girls (Pauline Parker was sixteen and Juliet Hulme was fifteen), the intensity of their friendship (with lesbian undertones), the brutal nature of the murder, and the revelations about their unconventional families were all factors that led to the murder being intensely publicised.[27] What dark forces were at play in such a green and pleasant city?

On 22 June 1954 the two girls had lunch with Pauline's family, then took Pauline's mother Honora out for afternoon tea at Victoria Park. There they bashed her to death with half a brick placed inside a stocking. Afterwards they ran back up to the Victoria Park tea kiosk, claiming that Pauline's mother had fallen and hurt her head.[28] Two months later they were found guilty of murder.

Author Peter Graham has argued that, in part due to the film, 'the murder is internationally New Zealand's most famous crime'.[29] For most people, the Christchurch location of the so-called 'Parker–Hulme murder' is incidental. It is a story of matricide, post-Second World War moral panic and a 'folie a deux' between two very close young women. But is that all? Many Cantabrians have always wondered how such a dreadful crime could happen in the place represented in the 1952 publicity film. Peter Graham has gone so far as to suggest that:

> The Parker–Hulme murder was somehow embedded in the soil of Christchurch, as much a part of local history as the pilgrims who, a century earlier, had footed it over the bridle path from Lyttelton, the men in frockcoats and top hats, the women in crinolines, to found the city.[30]

The point is well made: the murder has all kinds of resonances and interpretations in relation to Christchurch as a place. Juliet Hulme appeared to represent all things English. Both the school she attended at the time of the murder, and her home, Ilam Homestead, appear in the 1952 publicity film. A well-known photograph taken of her shortly before the murder has her posing amongst azaleas. Feminist historians Alison Laurie and Julie Glamuzina devote the first chapter of their 1991 book, *Parker and Hulme: A Lesbian View*, to the place that Christchurch was. They emphasise the English, white, conservative, heterosexist and class-ridden aspects of Christchurch at the time.[31] The Christchurch context is also lurking behind Peter Graham's interpretation when he writes: 'A few days before Xmas 1950, while Christchurch was celebrating the centenary of the arrival of the first four ships of the Canterbury Association in 1850, the Hulmes had a party at Ilam.'[32]

Graham explicitly links Christchurch's post-war identity to Englishness, writing that 'The Englishness of Christchurch and Canterbury was both an article of faith and a source of pride for many who lived there.' But he is also clear that 'it was, of course, a caricature: the inhabitants of Christchurch were no more typified by rich, jolly, anglified sheep farmers than Londoners were by Beefeaters and duchesses in tiaras', and notes of Christchurch's suburbs that 'it took a good deal of wishful thinking to see anything much of old England'.[33] In post-quake Christchurch, there are lessons in Graham's interpretation. The suggestion of a past English identity now prompts a strong nostalgic feeling that is associated with fear, loss and change, rather than a desire to understand the complexity of the past.

If the Englishness of 1950s Christchurch represents a benevolent aspect of the city's Gothic identity, the Parker–Hulme murder reveals its darker side. Adding to the literal Gothic tone of the crime, the trial played out at the Christchurch Supreme Court, a neo-Gothic building built in drab grey stone with a 'somber interior [that] seemed designed to intimidate all who had business there'.[34] The Gothic undertones are further noted by Joanne Drayton when she describes Juliet's time at Auckland's Mount Eden Prison: 'With massive grey stone walls, ugly Colonial Gothic castellations, and menacing watch-towers, it was the perfect expression of a prison designed to punish'.[35]According to Drayton, at fifteen years old, Anne Perry found herself living in a world reminiscent of Gothic horror fiction, where prisoners were hanged and her health suffered as her wisdom teeth became impacted and abscessed.[36]

During the Canterbury earthquakes a monument in Bromley's Ruru Lawn Cemetery to the forty-one victims of another bleak disaster in the city's history was badly damaged. Like the Parker–Hulme murder, the fire in the J. Ballantyne and Company department store in the central city on 18 November 1947 cast a long Gothic shadow over the city. A subsequent royal commission found that an overwhelmed fire service arrived too late, and there were delays in evacuating the building and breaches of building safety. Many victims were young women who worked on the upper floors and were trapped.[37]

Repairing the damaged Ballantyne monument was not straightforward. With the Halswell Quarry where the stone for the monument had come from closed, finding new material to fix the structure was going to be difficult. Luckily Buzz March of

March Construction came to the rescue, donating stone that he had stored for over thirty years. His Halswell Quarry stone was salvaged from the Supreme Court when it was demolished. The Parker–Hulme murder trial, the Ballantyne fire and the earthquakes – three dark moments in the history of the city – were thus linked.[38]

Vital in both contemporary and later accounts of the murder of Honora Parker has been the issue of morals. The crime occurred at a time of nationwide 'moral panic' about the behaviour of teenagers, who were thought to be challenging and threatening social order. On the basis of much-publicised reports of scandalous sexual behaviour among youths in Petone, near Wellington, a Special Committee on Moral Delinquency in Children and Adolescents (the Mazengarb Committee) was set up in 1954 by the government. The committee's report of September 1954 was distributed free to every New Zealand family. It recommended various measures, including more censorship and preventing access to contraceptives by young people, to stop what it saw as a decline in moral values.[39] According to Peter Graham, 'To many the evil act of Parker and Hulme was a prime example of the moral rot afflicting adolescents.' Furthermore, 'To somber citizens, the fetid secret lives of Pauline Parker and Juliet Hulme were clear evidence of a sickness infecting youth.'[40] Laurie and

Glamuzina placed the murder of Honora Parker in the social context of mid-1950s New Zealand and its rigid views on sexuality and social control. They argued that the trial of Pauline Parker and Juliet Hulme contributed to the widespread association of lesbianism with 'evil', 'insanity' and murder, and in general reinforced negative attitudes about lesbianism.[41]

What was it that so tragically brought two girls together into such an ultimately destructive relationship? Both girls came from unconventional families, and this was made much of in press reports of the trial. According to Joanne Drayton, 'There was nothing straight-thinking or normal ... about the lives of the adults involved in this tragedy.'[42] The murder investigation revealed that Honora Parker was not married to her partner, who had settled in Christchurch with her after deserting his wife in the North Island. At the trial Pauline's sister Rosemary, who had Down syndrome, was also mentioned as a way of signalling the family's difference.[43] Juliet's mother Hilda Hulme was in the process of leaving her husband, and her lover Bill Perry accompanied her to the trial. Peter Graham convincingly argues that both girls probably had personality disorders and were socially and morally detached from society. Pauline lived in a sleepout at the back of a ramshackle house in the inner city where her parents took in boarders to make ends meet. She cast herself as misunderstood and an outsider. She had suffered from osteomyelitis as a five-year-old and had a permanent limp. Juliet was from a privileged background and lived in the luxurious Ilam Homestead. She had endured the Blitz in London, suffered periods of separation from her mother, and after contracting pneumonia at the end of the war had been sent to Barbados to recuperate. She was reunited with her parents in Christchurch in 1948 when Henry Hulme became rector at Canterbury University College. After attending St Margaret's College, she was sent away to school in Hawke's Bay, returning to Christchurch to attend Christchurch Girls' High School where she met Pauline Parker.[44] At fourteen she again suffered bad health, this time contracting tuberculosis, and spent almost four months in a sanatorium while her parents were in London.

By the end of 1953 the girls were fast friends. Then in early 1954 Henry Hulme was forced to resign from the university. With his marriage disintegrating, Hulme decided to return to the United Kingdom; Juliet would go to stay with an aunt in South Africa until her health improved. Meanwhile, Pauline's mother attempted to put the brakes on what she had come to consider an unhealthy relationship between the girls, who were distraught at their looming separation. Henry Hulme placated them by promising to write to

Honora Parker to ask if Pauline could accompany Juliet to South Africa, but there is no evidence of his doing so, and the idea was far-fetched. The girls, meanwhile, came to see Honora as the obstacle to their being together. Their plan to 'moider mother' was hatched, carefully planned and tragically executed.

Why, then, have Pauline Parker and Juliet Hulme been seen by some in more recent decades as alternative heroines – youthful free spirits, who challenged Christchurch's societal and sexual norms? Was the city's proud but stifling conservatism responsible for their immersion in an imaginary world that made them capable of committing the crime? That could be one interpretation of *Heavenly Creatures*. Bill Pearson's 1952 essay about New Zealand society and culture, 'Fretful Sleepers', captured the post-war climate of small-society conformity. His biographer Paul Millar suggests that Pearson understood Christchurch well as he lived there in 1947–48 while studying for a Master of Arts at Canterbury University College.[45] Pearson's experiences of Christchurch surely made a central contribution to his essay. English novelist Fay Weldon, who spent some of her childhood years in Christchurch, would later describe post-war New Zealand as 'repressive and repressed'.[46] Julie Glamuzina and Alison Laurie, while stopping short of depicting the girls as alternative rebels, write: 'Clearly, for some observers, much lay under the surface of the apparently "respectable" Christchurch.'[47] They offer a sympathetic reading of the crime that places much weight on the Christchurch context and focuses on how the event affected the lives of all lesbians. More recently, decentring the murder itself from her discussion, Nadia Gush draws on the ideas of twentieth-century French philosopher Jacques Derrida to argue that it was the girls' subversive friendship that was on trial.[48]

The dark Gothic as a threatening, illegal homosexuality was a part of post-war Christchurch. Chris Brickell has written about the lives of gay men in Christchurch during and after the Second World War. He argues that there were 'circles of friends' that were 'the precursors to New Zealand's gay activist organisations of the later decades', suggesting that 'without the earlier development of social networks, the more formal push for equality could not have happened'.[49] There could be dangers. For example, David Wildey had an attic flat on the corner of Kilmore Street and Park Terrace. In 1964 Charles (Allan) Aberhart was at Wildey's flat with friends for lunch; afterwards he went to Hagley Park and was murdered.[50] Six youths aged fifteen to seventeen were found not guilty when they used the defence that Aberhart had provoked them by making a sexual advance.[51] After the murder

Wildey moved to Auckland. This story reveals a latent homophobic climate in Christchurch that was challenged in private and helps put the Parker-Hulme case in context.

Heavenly Creatures has offered a version of events and a view of Christchurch that has served to perpetuate the blurring between fact, fiction and fantasy. Maureen Molloy has interpreted the film as evoking the uncanny – the eerie, weird, gruesome, frightening, familiar yet strange – which is transposed onto Christchurch of the time. Writing in the mid-1990s, Molloy considered the cultural reproduction of Honora Parker in the 1990s to be uncanny. She argues that the nation had become obsessed with dead women.[52]

Other films have gone much further than Walsh and Jackson in *Heavenly Creatures*, blending fact, fiction and fantasy to explain and even celebrate the murder. Various amateur commentators have merged and blended photos of Parker and Hulme with photos of the actresses who played them, Melanie Lynskey and Kate Winslet. One such montage, 'Juliet's Panic', implies that the murder had to do with Hulme's reaction to living in Christchurch. It ends with a photo of the adult Juliet Hulme and the words 'the killer grin' – somehow coquettish, romantic and celebratory. Mario Lanza's 'Be My Love', a song favoured by the girls, provides the sound track to the mash-up.

The girls appear as heroic cult figures, rebels with a cause, full of the heady success of their evil – and even, disturbingly, worthy of fans.

The lives of Parker and Hulme have continued to be unsettling. While Juliet served five and a half years at Mount Eden Prison, Pauline was incarcerated at Arohata Prison. After her release Pauline changed her name to Hilary Nathan, working as a librarian in New Zealand and a teacher in Kent before moving to Orkney in Scotland. A devout Catholic who worked with special-needs children, she also painted murals on her cottage wall of two mystical figures said to resemble Parker and Hulme. Juliet became Anne Perry, spent time in California, and became a Mormon. She also became famous as a crime writer. When the release of *Heavenly Creatures* led to their previous identities being uncovered, it was Juliet who reluctantly spoke, while Pauline remained silent. Joanne Drayton's 2012 book about Anne Perry rehabilitates her, ironically through her writing of crime fiction. Drayton believes that:

> Anne Perry explains herself in her writing, in the stories of flawed protagonists who fail the world and themselves but can transcend their past to find forgiveness. They battle their history, the corrupting influences of the world and their own fallibility and self-doubt … And until the world finally 'gets it', and she can forgive

herself, it is a story she will tell over and over again.[53]

The crime remains chilling and its effects bleak, irreversibly affecting the lives of the families of both girls, and remaining in Christchurch's consciousness. Years later, around the time of the release of *Heavenly Creatures*, the same Christchurch Girls' High School building which featured in the film became infamous through another court case. In 1992 early childhood education teacher Peter Ellis and four women colleagues, who worked at the Christchurch Civic Creche in the former school building complex, were charged with sexually abusing children in their care. There was much hysteria and sensationalism in the media, and some of the allegations made had occultish overtones. Charges against the women were dropped, but Peter Ellis was convicted and spent seven years in prison. He was released in 2000, still maintaining his innocence, and by this time had considerable support.[54] The case was controversial and frightening, with the evidence given appearing to combine fact with fantasy, bringing to mind the diaries of Pauline Parker. The dark side of Christchurch's Gothic imagination was back.

In the radically altered landscape of Christchurch, the good Gothic of Englishness and the garden city and the dark Gothic have both ruptured. What happens next in the post-apocalyptic city will likely demonstrate that truth can be stranger than fiction. The time is right to think carefully about what values and moods architectural styles signal and evoke. And more than ever, there is the opportunity to learn from the past and to create a safe city that adequately cares for its citizens and that turns its back on fear and repression.

5. HEART

Christchurch's inner city has dramatically changed for ever. The debate over the future of the Anglican cathedral epitomises the rupture. As Christchurch's best-known landmark, positioned at the historical heart of the city, the cathedral has become a symbolic marker of the devastation that took place between 2011 and 2012, as well as a symbol of hope for the future. No one died in the cathedral during the earthquakes, and this has added potency to its presence as a sanctuary, rather than as a pile of deadly masonry condemned to the wrecking ball.

The 'cathedral debate' is located in the space between heritage and history. It reveals the differences between those who want to recreate the past, those who want a wholly new future for the building and the city, and those who are indifferent. Nostalgia is understandably strong during times of disaster and loss, but as the cathedral's pragmatic Anglican Church owner is aware, the past the cathedral represents is over, and much has changed in post-quake times. It is time to think outside of the square. This chapter looks at the ruptured centre or heart. After the Canterbury earthquakes, the centre of the city was 'red-zoned', closed and damaged. The broken Anglican cathedral symbolises the disaster, yet also the hope for the city's renewal. Its representation, and the controversy and debate over its future, is analysed in relation to Christchurch's 'broken heart'. While American and global influences were a pre-quake reality in Christchurch, the Canterbury earthquakes have given suburbanisation in the style of the late twentieth-century subdivisions and commuter towns a boost. 'Gap fillers' and alternative activities have emerged in the city centre, but new housing developments evoke 1970s suburban living rather than new forms of relevant and creative urban planning. Heritage buildings were rapidly demolished, signalling a return to the blank slate ideology of the mid-nineteenth century.

At its most general and symbolic, the cathedral has come to mean 'Christchurch' as a generic place marker. Indeed, for many the Christ Church Cathedral exists merely as an icon with good branding potential – an image to be placed on a letterhead, stamped on a wheelie bin, and of course featured on a whole host of souvenirs. It proclaims 'Christchurch' in all its multiplicity of meanings, promising everything and nothing at once. Since the quakes, images of the broken cathedral have saturated the media and have been used in a variety of ways: an advertisement for New Zealand Insurance on 'Restoring Canterbury', for example, featured the shattered cathedral.[1] There are many diverse feelings, ideas and ownership claims. Deciding that the cathedral should live on, citizens have in very personal fashion created embodied memorials by tattooing its rose window on their arms, rebuilding models of the cathedral out of Lego, and crafting cathedral necklaces and rose window earrings.

As with the region in general, the Christ Church Cathedral was subjected to an on-going pounding from the series of Canterbury earthquakes, each resulting in further damage and prompting a rethink of options. On 4 September 2010 the cathedral was damaged, but was afterwards cleared for occupancy. Then on 22 February 2011 it suffered major damage, especially to the spire and part of the tower. The aftershocks of 13 June 2011 caused further significant damage: the rose window was destroyed and the west wall collapsed. Discussion moved on more firmly to demolition and deconsecration. Aftershocks on 23 December

2011 caused further weakening. In March 2012 the tower was reduced to a safe level.

A random poll in a local newspaper in November 2011 captured the diversity of opinions about the cathedral's future. When asked what its fate should be, Bernie Wood, an orchardist from South Brighton, responded: 'Of course it should be bashed down, and so should the Catholic one too, those buildings are a terrible waste of space and just ornamental.' Anna Moore, a student living in Riccarton, agreed, saying, 'It should be demolished.' On the other hand, Karen Smythe, a laboratory technician from Kaiapoi, believed that 'it is a Christchurch icon and one of the few things in Christchurch which should be restored'. Bob Duncan, an electrician from Pegasus Town, was of the same view: 'It should be kept and restored.' Andrew Grenon, a musician from Edgeware, thought that 'the decision-making on the ultimate solution should be by the Cathedral diocese and not central government'. Hamish West, a student living in Riccarton, was happy for the cathedral to be restored, 'but not at the taxpayers' cost'.[2]

As we have seen, a feature of New Zealand's colonial settlement was to start with a blank slate. In Christchurch, Captain Thomas and his assistant Edward Jollie set about naming the streets with familiar old-world reference points, clearly placing Christchurch within the British Empire. The

Anglican cathedral in the central square clearly symbolised imperialism. Before the Canterbury earthquakes, however, economic restructuring had seen the artisan roots of the city and its key role as an agricultural service town transformed.[3] The central city had become an important tourism site, with the area within the four avenues taking on the character of a colonial theme park featuring neo-Gothic architecture, statues and gardens. With ever-increasing suburbanisation, the growth of shopping malls and the retreat of the state to Wellington, tourism had really saved Cathedral Square: buildings were reused as hotels, backpackers' accommodation and apartments. The post office became a visitor information centre, and even the cathedral built a visitor centre and café. Cathedral Square had become what we might term post-modern – that is, self-consciously promoting and selling its history to visitors, rather than functioning as the hub of the modern city.

If the cathedral was a key symbolic place marker, how better for the city to rise again than by rebuilding it? There are many who look beyond the image and who wish to preserve the building because of its place in the city's heritage or its commercial value as a tourist attraction, just as there are others who would like it reconsecrated as a place of interfaith worship, and those who would like it retained half-ruined as a memorial.

Sustained since the earthquakes and constantly in the public eye with new developments over its future, the broken Anglican cathedral has generated an outpouring of emotions. For example, in June 2014 the *Star* was deluged with a mix of impassioned responses to a column by Chris Lynch in favour of demolition.[4] And when the *Press* reported on 18 March 2015 that Anglican Church authorities were considering a compromise plan to rebuild with wood in a modern neo-Gothic design by architect Sir Miles Warren, it received more than sixty letters to the editor.

Soon after the quakes, there had been a call to expand the Anglican cathedral into a multi-faith space that better recognised Christchurch's twenty-first-century population. Alan Goss, a Napier-based former Presbyterian minister, called for a 'people's cathedral' that could be shared by many religions. Art historian Jonathan Mane-Wheoki said that it was already a people's cathedral because of the number of activities that took place there. At the same time, he emphasised that the cathedral was a reminder of the city's Anglican origins. Dean of the cathedral, Peter Beck, responded that a multi-faith rebuild was unlikely, reaffirming the use of the site prior to the earthquakes: 'It's a holy place, a sacred space for all people of all faiths, [but] at the heart of it, it is a Christian church. It's the Anglican's cathedral.'[5]

Built heritage advocates favouring the restoration of the cathedral argue their case on a number of fronts. Architectural historian Ian Lochhead notes that the cathedral is 'in the very heart of the city', and is 'the enduring symbol of the special nature of the Canterbury Association's idealistic colonising venture'. Suggesting progress into the future through recollection of past founders, he argues for the perpetuation of the values of the Canterbury settlement, with the cathedral demonstrating 'what a community of a few thousand people could achieve through sacrifice, dedication and hard work'. For Lochhead, 'the city and its centrally placed cathedral are one', and he articulates an Anglican hegemony that the Anglican Church would likely neither agree with nor push, even it felt safe to do so. He suggests that 'Buildings such as Christ Church Cathedral are the embodiment of the aspirations of an entire community.'[6] Heritage advocate Haydn Rawstron of Lansdown conflates the cathedral's potential for tourism and commerce and its heritage and spiritual value. He urges '[r]estore the cathedral, our most powerful brand', and continues '[r]estoration would also give the Anglican Church its best chance, since 1850, again to fulfil its Cantabrian destiny, selflessly and in Christian spirit, for the greater good.'[7]

When the cathedral suffered further damage in the earthquakes of June 2011, uncertainty about the timing of a rebuild was replaced by uncertainty as to whether the cathedral would be rebuilt at all. The prominent rose window was destroyed and discussion had moved on to consider deconsecration and demolition. Thinking pragmatically rather than emotionally as the rupture to the centre became clearer, the Anglican Church articulated the city's changed geography. Bishop Victoria Matthews said '[w]e want to be in the centre of the city as an icon', and commented that the church would move west if the centre of the city shifted west. She pointed out that the city's needs had changed significantly since the mid-nineteenth century and said that any new cathedral would be built to serve current needs. Dean Peter Beck concurred: 'The Cathedral in the Square has been in the heart of our city almost from the beginning, but wherever the heart of the city is, that is where we will be'.[8]

Discussion on the heart of the city in mid-2011 brought forth a wide range of opinions. A. C. Mitton of Strowan suggested a science centre for Cathedral Square. Richard Dingle of Belfast advocated Hagley Park as the city's heart and continued 'May I suggest the cathedral either stays where it is or it goes to where the people are, say in the poorer suburbs where the need is great, not sitting at the most prominent part of the table, so to speak. Some humility would go a long way.'[9] In June 2011,

Fletchers Construction Company placed a large advertisement in the *Press*, claiming that 'New Zealand's world famous historic garden city needs the right people to help rebuild it to its former glory.' It chose a picture of the Catholic cathedral to capture its intentions.[10]

In May 2011, The 'Rise Up Christchurch' global telethon used the sculpture *Chalice* in Cathedral square as its logo.[11] Neil Dawson's sculpture mirrors the spire of Christ Church Cathedral, and incorporates shapes from the building with the leaves of forty-two native tree species that grew in the area – suggesting a city that is grounded in its history, but that also grows out of its natural environment. *Chalice* was intended to harmonise the past and the future, celebrating the new millennium and commemorating the 150th anniversary of the founding of Christchurch and Canterbury by the Canterbury Association.[12] Foreshadowing post-quake debates, there was strong public interest in the sculpture and its central placement. In addition, the moderate intentions of *Chalice* didn't stop some from viewing it as an offensive eyesore – a further harbinger of post-quake opposition to change and innovation.

Following the first of the quakes, the Anglican Church found itself in ownership of a sacred site subject to many civil claims. As a result it has had to proceed with extreme caution in a highly charged situation. This was made particularly difficult because of the Canterbury Earthquake Regional Authority's strategy of attempting to facilitate rapid and pragmatic city recovery. Most seriously, on 28 October 2011 CERA issued the Church with a section 38 notice, giving it ten days to advise on its plans to make the building safe. The Anglicans submitted plans on 8 November. At this time, twenty-seven Christchurch heritage buildings had been demolished, despite Heritage New Zealand (formerly the New Zealand Historic Places Trust) recommending they be saved. Anna Crighton, Heritage New Zealand trust board member and Christchurch heritage advocate, said, 'History will show just what a huge mistake we have made, ripping out our city heart.'[13]

The Canterbury Earthquake Recovery Act had, however, reduced Heritage New Zealand's power to an advisory role. This meant that heritage buildings such as Cranmer Courts (the neo-Gothic Normal School that was successfully converted into apartments in the 1980s), the children's library, the Guthrey building façade and the Zetland building were able to be demolished. In September 2011 Christchurch Central MP Brendon Burns called the trust 'gutless' in its advocacy for Christchurch heritage, arguing that a number of these demolished buildings could have been saved.[14] Directly after the 22 February earthquakes Gerry Brownlee, MP for Ilam and minister in charge of the earthquake recovery, described some Christchurch buildings as 'old dungers' that needed to be pulled down as soon as possible.[15] In the heat of the moment, he effectively denied the importance of history in building the future city. His comments were taken to signal carte blanche for the bulldozer. Brendon Burns became an advocate for the restoration of heritage buildings, including the cathedral, stating 'If there is one building I think we should try to rebuild to the new code, damaged though it may be, it is our cathedral.'[16]

In response to CERA, the Anglican Church took the intermediate step of deconsecrating the cathedral on 9 November 2011. This paved the way for the partial demolition of the building to make it safe while longer-term options were considered.[17] The deconsecration precipitated another outpouring of opinion. There was a xenophobic reaction to Bishop Victoria Matthews. A letter that won the *Press*'s 'letter of the week' suggested that the Bishop did not understand the city and should return to her Canadian homeland.[18] Others, like Anglican Milton Hayward of Shirley, wrote in support of the Bishop, arguing that 'It's cowardly to play it safe and cling to the past. Be brave, seize the moment, pioneer a new direction and do something special.' Hayward used the Sydney Opera House as a daring but successful example of thinking outside the square.[19] Tanya Malcolm of Shirley wrote: 'How could we justify spending $50 million restoring a cathedral when so many people in the world are starving and homeless?'[20] There were diverse and conflicting opinions, both in the community and the Anglican Church.

A *Press* editorial at the time suggested that 'The challenge for the Anglican Church as it wrestles with the financial implications of a rebuild, is that the wider community feels the cathedral belongs to the whole city.'[21] This view was articulated by Peter Ross of Heathcote who wrote: 'To those like me who were born, grew up and have lived out our lives here the cathedral was not particularly a church. It was the hub of the city. It was the icon by which Christchurch recognised itself and by which others recognised Christchurch.' Ross added that the Bishop 'is not a sufficient part of Christchurch that she should be making decisions about the Cathedral'. On the other hand, Daryl Cotterell pointed out the partiality of these arguments, writing that no one seemed to be making a fuss about the badly damaged Roman Catholic basilica.[22]

It was Dean Peter Beck rather than Bishop Matthews who resigned after the deconsecration to stand as a candidate in the Burwood–Pegasus Ward by-election of February 2012. He was sworn in at a meeting of the Christchurch City Council on 23 February 2012.[23] Bishop Matthews stood resolute, telling the *Press* in December 2011, '[t]hey can tell me to go back to Canada as often as they like. I'm not leaving,' and saying, 'I have been treated pretty shabbily. I have a ministry to serve, and rude letters are not going to send me packing. I think a lot less of Kiwi hospitality than I did earlier.' In the face of disaster the Church also was steadfast and pragmatic. It remained cautious about deciding on the cathedral's fate while waiting for the complete engineering reports, and attempted to take the focus off the cathedral by pointing out that a total of twenty-four Anglican churches were damaged or destroyed. As Bishop Matthews said, 'It doesn't feel good that all the spotlight is on the cathedral any more than it would feel good if a house in Fendalton was always being talked about when there were hundreds of houses broken in the eastern suburbs.'[24]

After further damage to the cathedral during the strong aftershocks on 23 December 2011, in February 2012 the Anglican Church placed a half-page advertisement in the Saturday *Press*; it included images that emphasised the extent of the damage to the cathedral and a statement from Bishop Matthews about the cathedral's future. She wrote that buildings, 'however dear to our heart and beautiful, are secondary to our concern for people. At this time we are especially aware of those who suffered injuries on 22 February 2011 and the families of those who died on that tragic day. … We are also aware that the Church is the people and not the buildings'.[25] A decision on the cathedral's future was to be announced in March 2012 after new engineering assessments. Downplaying the spiritual, the Church appeared mindful of the complex and pressing needs of its community, aware of a dwindling congregation and resigned to the fact the city had changed for ever.

As noted in Chapter 3, one unexpected result of the earthquakes was that it was the Wizard of New Zealand, and not the Anglican Bishop of Christchurch, who was constantly involved in campaigns to save Christ Church Cathedral. As early as April 2011, the Wizard called for the city to turn 'to the gothic vision of the Canterbury pilgrims for inspiration'.[26] In mid-2011 he took out a half-page advertisement in the *Press* titled 'A statement from the Wizard of Christchurch', claiming ownership of the cathedral and advocating its restoration. He claimed: 'The Cathedral is not just property, whether of the Anglican Diocese or the City Council. It is the most important material part of our history as a people and we are all its custodians.' He accused the Church authorities of wanting to destroy the cathedral and suggested handing over ownership to the people of Christchurch – effectively what some citizens had already done in their minds. He promised to cast a 'gothic revival' spell to stop threatened demolition. An important Christchurch tourist attraction himself, the Wizard considered that his spell would 'also help preserve Christchurch as a vitally important cultural destination for tourists. We are going to need tourist income more than ever before, otherwise our city will wither and die. We simply can't afford to lose any more.'[27] The scale of the repairs needed, however, was overwhelming.

Christchurch's heritage movement, of which the Wizard is a part, advocates appreciation and restoration of historic places for the good of the present and the future, clearly indicated in the name of the heritage lobby group IConIC – Interests in Conserving the Identity of Christchurch. As noted in Chapter 3, the Great Christchurch Buildings Trust, including conservative Phillip Burdon and radical Jim Anderton, argued that the cathedral represented the city and its centre, and the heart of the people, and asserted that the owners were the caretakers for all the citizens. They too argued that the cathedral was a 'financial magnet for tourism and business in Christchurch', and that '[i]t also has a powerful significance for many of the residents of the city, as both a secular image and a spiritual heart.' They believed that demolishing the cathedral would be 'financial and marketing suicide for any city that values its future investment in its emotional heart, international identity, cultural heritage, business and tourism'.[28]

When in March 2012 the Church sought to demolish the walls of the cathedral down to a safe level, the Great Christchurch Buildings Trust took the Anglican Church Property Trustees to court, seeking an injunction to stop the demolition. That court case and the battery of others that followed all failed legally, but they effectively caused a deadlock, placing the future of the cathedral in limbo, with no one able to make a decision. In May 2012 a disappointed Jim Anderton said that public funds had been used to build the cathedral and so it belonged to the people.[29] Despite the legal defeat, the heritage lobby was on a roll. IConIC, the Great Christchurch Buildings Trust and the Restore Christchurch Cathedral Campaign came together for a rally, asserting: 'We citizens are tired and weary but we must fight to save our heritage history and heart.' The emphasis was on saving and restoring the cathedral, without drawing on ratepayer money, so that 'the emotional heart of the city' would remain intact. The aim was for 'the Christchurch Cathedral to be a symbol of our courage and hope, our city's identity, our culture and our heritage'.[30] A long legal battle was under way.

In April 2013, the Anglican Church released three options for the future of the cathedral: restoration, a new traditional rebuild, and a contemporary rebuild.[31] Shigeru Ban's Transitional Cathedral, the world's only cathedral made substantially of cardboard, opened in August 2013 at 234 Hereford Street, just east of Cathedral Square.[32] Implementing new post-quake visions in the face of opposition was, however, difficult. In respect of plans for a more permanent cathedral, there were signs of compromise. For example in 2011, Canterbury architect Sir Miles Warren said in response to the Wizard's calls for restoration that rebuilding the cathedral in neo-Gothic style was 'non-sense' and that the building would be structurally unsound. He said he wanted to see the best contemporary architecture employed, as had happened after the 1931 Hawke's Bay earthquake when Benjamin Mountfort's neo-Gothic cathedral of St John's, Napier (1888) was rebuilt in Spanish style.[33] Yet in March 2015, in an about-turn, a neo-Gothic design by Sir Miles in wood with a copper roof was released as a way forward.[34]

Anglicans, themselves divided, attempted to come to grips with the civil takeover of their space. John Bluck, formerly Dean of the cathedral for twelve years, wrote that he was baffled by the 'public outcry and media storm' over the cathedral's future and by the ferocity of the debate concerning the outside of the building 'with so little reference to the inside of the building and what actually happened there'.[35] Recalling that the Wizard had visited only to leave his ladder in the tower, Bluck wrote that 'unless they've had a radical change of heart, some of the loudest voices were never heard or seen inside the building when I was there'. For Bluck, the post-quake cathedral had become a symbol of 'great expectations', and the debate revealed that the connections Cantabrians made with the building 'were not often very religious and never exclusively Anglican'.[36]

The Reverend John Latham also challenged the Wizard's position: 'I can understand the attraction of a mock Gothic parish to an Englishman who specialises in a mock antiquarian activity,' he wrote, but the cathedral had 'had its day'. He acknowledged the grief of losing the cathedral, but believed that denial was not the answer. The building was no longer 'fit for purpose', and the cardboard cathedral was better. For Latham, '[c]athedrals were not built to provide a scenic wonder'; he looked forward to a new 'visually inspiring' but practical building.[37]

A cluster of other correspondents made a similar point. In a 2015 'letter of the week' to the editor of the *Press,* Max Broadbent argued that 'Most of the people who have spoken or written about the Anglican cathedral have had nothing at all to say about Anglican worship.' He continued:

By contrast, the noisy critics of the Anglican authorities have been banging on about symbols, spiritual hearts, memorials of the war dead, of the earthquake dead, of pioneers, of ancestors. They say they want a venue for welcoming distinguished visitors to the city, for funerals of distinguished New Zealanders, for flower shows, for jazz nights, for visiting royal personages, for pet blessing ceremonies, for Anzac parades.[38]

The contest and stalemate over the cathedral's future has effectively rendered it a visible ruin, for citizens and visitors alike. Retaining it as a ruin was for long favoured by some who saw the cathedral as symbolising Christchurch. Former mayor Bob Parker appreciated the cathedral as an icon, but argued that with the city 'ripped apart' change was inevitable. He suggested combining parts of the old cathedral, encased in glass, with an alluring grand design, reminiscent of Coventry's combination of the new and old.[39] Others such as Dan Tobin supported keeping it as a ruin, suggesting that the shattered, steeple-less cathedral was the ultimate Canterbury earthquake symbol. Mark Fletcher added, 'Think of all the battered and broken icons around the world that stand proud, on their original sites', and mentioned the Parthenon, Stonehenge and the Colosseum.[40] And Colin Meurk suggested that leaving the iconic cathedral in ruins would be an appropriate memorial to the city's events and suffering.[41] But leaving the remains of the cathedral open to the elements was hastening disintegration. In May 2015, Heritage New Zealand supported a plan to build a $60,000 steel structure around it to arrest further deterioration.[42]

In the post-quake milieu, vital pieces of the city's fabric have faded into the background as the cathedral has taken centre stage. Well before the quakes the waning appeal and vibrancy of Cathedral Square was a lively topic for discussion. The city was evolving, embracing the motor car, turning towards the airport and copying modern American and Australian cities. The reality was not a neo-Gothic village. Cathedral Square, along with the Arts Centre, had become an historic precinct and a drawcard for tourists, rather than the central hub of a living city.

Cathedral Square itself is a place rich in history, from the creche and women's restrooms, to the six cinemas that opened between 1915 and 1930, to the four lanes leading in and out. In the 1990s, Therese Minehan and her team of women from the local history committee of the Canterbury branch of the Federation of University Women recovered and documented the history of its built environment. *Round the Square* reveals that Christchurch's heart was an ever-changing hub for commerce, entertainment, public service and transportation, as well as worship. The Square was the home to several life insurance offices, many government departments, a bank and two newspapers. Religion and commemoration co-existed with entertainment and business.[43] The Square's pulse altered with the changing time of day and the seasons. Pubs, cinemas, fast-food outlets and hairdressers were part of the pre-earthquake mix. And everybody was free to loiter there, leading to the appearance of many colourful characters besides the Wizard. The photographs in David Cook's 2014 exhibition *Meet Me in the Square* capture the unsanitised, diverse and edgy place that it was during the 1980s.[44] In his review of Cook's exhibition and book, cultural historian Redmer Yska adds that the dangerous, repellent and miserable were also elements in the Square's identities.[45]

Post-quake Christchurch is abruptly crafting a new topography. A change of heart, necessitated by the red zone that closed the area until June 2013, is evident in the forced post-quake relocation to the suburbs. Spaces beyond Cathedral Square have been used and reused in a whole range of safe, creative and exploratory ways. Businesses operate out of any available rooms; shops, bars and cafés have sprung up in shipping containers. You can have your hair cut or your passport photo taken or buy antiques in suburban garages. You can go to church in a tent and watch a film being screened on a wall while sitting in a gap created by a demolition.

An important indicator of the change in the heart of the city is that the number of people working in central Christchurch (that is, within the four avenues) halved between 2006 and 2013, from 39,213 to 19,419. Sales workers were down by 62.4 per cent, clerical and administrative workers by 64.2 per cent, managers by 57.4 per cent, and professionals by 35.4 per cent. Meanwhile, the areas with the biggest increases in workplaces were Middleton, Riccarton South and Addington (just outside the south-west edge of the four avenues, and widely regarded as unfashionable prior to the quakes), and Yaldhurst, Islington, Russley, Hornby North and Avonhead West (to the west of Christchurch city near the airport). Numbers of professionals, clerical and administrative workers and managers all increased in these areas.[46] Symbolic of the new geography, the long-established – some might say 'establishment' – Court Theatre relocated from the central Arts Centre to a reused warehouse beside a railway line in Addington. The move was considered temporary, but the arrival of professional theatre at a site more associated with working-class Christchurch set a new pattern for the city.

The ruptured, largely empty city centre has also changed people's transport use patterns. In the immediate aftermath of the quakes, it became impossible to enter the red-zoned area, and traffic moved to the outskirts of the city. Now it is motor vehicles rather than the bicycles and trams of earlier decades that are defining twenty-first-century life in Christchurch. Roads have become less hospitable for bikes and people often commute longer distances and more convoluted routes to work. Unsurprisingly, the 2013 census revealed a significant increase in the number of people living in greater Christchurch who drove a company car, truck, or van to work: 12.6 per cent (or 27,489 people) drove a company vehicle, up 22.6 per cent from 22,428 people in 2006. This was much higher than the 2.4 per cent increase nationally over the same time period. Christchurch was a city of utes and white vans buzzing around different routes, avoiding the thousands of traffic cones.[47]

Conversely, the number of people travelling to work by bus in greater Christchurch had fallen to 5,526 (2.5 per cent) at the 2013 census, down from an already low 7,443 (3.5 per cent) in 2006. In 2013, 10,578 employed people (4.9 per cent) cycled to work (up 7.9 per cent), and 8,064 (3.7 per cent) walked or jogged (down 16.1 per cent). Nationally, there was a 16 per cent increase in those who cycled to work and a 0.6 per cent increase in those who walked or jogged.[48]

'Traffic bypassing the central city appears to have put thousands of extra vehicles a day onto other roads since the earthquakes,' wrote Tom Doudney in 2015. A review of Christchurch City Council and New Zealand Transport Agency traffic count data before and after the earthquakes by the *Star* showed big increases on some Christchurch roads, particularly on western roads and those that took traffic around the central city. City council assets and network unit manager Chris Gregory cautioned against drawing firm conclusions, as changes could be partly a continuation of pre-earthquake trends or natural variation. 'What is contributing to congestion is the wider distribution of destinations people are travelling to,' he said. He considered it 'highly unlikely' that traffic patterns would return to how they were before the earthquakes.'[49] The heart of the city was shut off, and the blood now pumped through different veins.

It is important to recognise, however, that change had been happening well before the earthquakes. At the beginning of the twenty-first century, the roads were increasingly clogged with cars, and shopping malls away from the city centre were going from strength to strength. The sea and rail transportation so vital in the colonial era had given way to an extensive roading network, and the airport was a central hub.

Christchurch was always a city of suburbs, including the older inner suburbs such as Richmond, Woolston, Addington, St Albans and Fendalton, and the outer suburbs of Parklands, Westmorland, Hyde Park, Northwood and Ferrymead. Over time, as the city grew outwards, new boroughs developed. For example, boroughs came into existence in Sydenham in 1877, St Albans in 1881, Linwood in 1883, Woolston in 1893 and Spreydon in 1911. The pattern was for boroughs then to be absorbed into the city, as happened in St Albans and Linwood in 1903, and Spreydon and Woolston in 1921. Sumner was a borough between 1891 and 1945, New Brighton between 1896 and 1941, and Riccarton between 1913 and 1989. Indeed, 1989 was a watershed year with the amalgamation into the city of Heathcote County, Paparua County, South-west Waimairi County and Lyttelton Borough.[50] Then there were the satellite towns or 'xurbs' (prosperous areas outside of the city's suburbs, also known as 'commuter towns' and 'bedroom communities'). Among them were Rolleston, Rangiora, Pegasus Town, Kaiapoi, Prebbleton, Lincoln, Tai Tapu and West Melton. These towns have grown in number since the earthquakes.

It is possible to list over eighty Christchurch suburbs. But what do they actually mean for people? Suburbs are jurisdictions – but they can have social, economic and cultural histories too. They draw their character, including class hierarchies, from a range of influences. Suburbs are no longer planned around churches; instead the physical environment, facilities and schools shape them. If the number of books on the history of schools in Christchurch can be seen as an indicator of identity, suburban distinctions often come from schools and their communities. Bruce Ansley's memoir of New Brighton, located on the edge of the Pacific Ocean as well as the edge of Christchurch, serves as an example of the connection between people and place.[51] He recalls the beach, streets and characters of the area. Yet it can be argued that many of Christchurch's suburbs, unlike New Brighton, lack a distinct character. Pre-quake Christchurch was a city with a strong centre and mainly dormitory suburbs. Suburban malls and local pubs and cafes were really only very late twentieth and early twenty-first century developments. It was the east–west split of the city, with affluence generally located in the west, that was brought into sharp relief by the earthquakes. The division was reinforced by the generally greater impact of the earthquakes in eastern areas.

Geographer Yi Fu Tuan wrote in the 1970s: 'Suburb is an ideal. To middle-income people in the developed western countries the word suggests a whole way of life in which the best of rural and urban living are combined without their defects.'[52] Historically, suburbs were formed with strong values and ideals. One prominent example is the garden city movement engineered by Ebenezer Howard; as discussed in Chapter 4, this character has now ruptured. Jane Bowron wrote in January

2012, 'It's hard to believe around the inner city and affected suburbs that this was once called the Garden City, where control-freak gardeners slavishly dug, weeded, watered and landscaped, trying to impose order on mother nature.'[53] Post-quake apocalypse had replaced the quarter acre pavlova paradise, a term for post-war New Zealand suburbia coined in 1972 by academic Austin Mitchell, who taught political science at the University of Canterbury before returning to the United Kingdom to become a politician.[54]

Compared with other countries New Zealand has avoided the worst excesses of city life, involving crime, filth and degradation, instead plumping for the dull conformity of suburbia. The term 'suburbia' was used to mock the ideal, signalling lack of fulfilment (particularly for women), boredom and conformity.[55] In the 1970s, writing generally about suburbs, Yi Fu Tuan argued that 'we remain largely ignorant of the quality and range of experience in different types of physical setting under different conditions'.[56] It appears that despite the very visceral experience of the Canterbury earthquakes, there has been little attempt subsequently to build new living environments. Instead, there is an air of pragmatic denial – of building on land packages in former fields, close to a main road for ease of to transport – because the city centre has changed. As Eric Pawson has written, suburbia in twentieth-century Christchurch, as elsewhere, was about a 'family lifestyle' that could be lived 'in surroundings that offered the prospect of beautification while shutting out the ills of the city'. By the 1990s, in the face of traffic congestion and the encroachment on good agricultural land, there were concerns about the future sustainability of suburbs.[57] In post-quake Christchurch there is a retrograde move to relocate to suburbs, and to build new ones. People understandably seek safety after trauma in fresh new housing developments. Struggling Pegasus Town, in Waimakariri district, was given a lifeline by the earthquakes. So too was Rolleston, located in the country's fastest-developing district of Selwyn.

The growth of xurbs provides plenty of evidence of the way Christchurch's centre has ruptured, and of new mobility patterns. For example, there was a 32.2 per cent increase in the number of people commuting into Christchurch city to work from Hurunui, Waimakariri, Selwyn and Ashburton districts. In 2013, 13.4 per cent of the Christchurch city workforce (23,166 people) commuted to work from surrounding districts – up from 17,526 (10.7 per cent) in 2006. There was an increase in the number of people commuting into Christchurch city from Selwyn district – 11,169 people (up 44 per cent) and Waimakariri district – 10,728 people (up 20.1 per cent). As well, there was a surge in the number of people commuting in the other direction:

3,807 people travelled from Christchurch city to Selwyn district (up 56.5 per cent), and 2,058 people to Waimakariri district (up 45.6 per cent).[58]

It was those driving a company vehicle who gravitated towards the xurbs, particularly in the Waimakariri and Selwyn districts. Probably they were able to live further away from their place of work as transportation costs were not a disincentive. In greater Christchurch, too, there were increases in those who drove a company vehicle to work. In Christchurch city, numbers were up 14.6 per cent; in Waimakariri district, up 40.3 per cent; and in Selwyn district, up 63.0 per cent.[59]

In post-quake Christchurch, retirement complexes are becoming an integral part of the new suburbs. There is a communal feeling about these developments, although they are a far cry from Alexander Bickerton's collective community ideas. One example is the planned 'Summerset at Wigram' village, owned by Summerset Group, the third largest operator and the second largest developer of retirement villages in New Zealand, with twenty villages across the country. This complex will occupy 5.4 hectares near the Wigram Skies development in the south-west of Christchurch. It is to consist of approximately 200 homes, with a mixture of stand-alone villas, townhouse and care apartments, along with a village centre and care centre. Advertising material emphasises that the village has 'good links to the southern Christchurch motorway and is just a five minute drive to Hornby Mall'.[60]

On the other side of town at the new Prestons subdivision on fertile marshland soil, the Alpine View Lifestyle Village is being built. Again, it offers five levels of care from independent villa to full resthome care, and weekly service fees start at $165. The services on offer include an indoor swimming pool, medical centre, bar, movie theatre, chapel, hair salon, restaurant, billiards room and library; an added bonus is that the government is building a new specialised aged care public hospital for Christchurch 'just down the road'. The vision at Alpine View is for 'excellent care, good security and each resident (and their accommodation) having their own special non-institutionalised identity. It is similar to a normal sub-division, with healthcare attached.'[61] It is over to the developers to determine residents' quality of life. And profit is the overall motivating factor.

Property developers and planners in post-quake Christchurch would do well to heed the words of Sister Pauline O'Regan. After many years as a school teacher, including seventeen years as principal of Villa Maria College, Sister Pauline, along with fellow nuns Teresa O'Connor and Helen Goggin, went to work in Aranui and East Christchurch in 1973. Their calling came after they had heard of 'the desperation of so many of the girls we had taught who had got married and shortly afterwards had started families in the suburbs. So many were lonely, desperate in their isolation.' Sister Pauline recalls:

> The developers were building whole new suburbs for young families with no infrastructure, no support mechanisms. When two of us later moved over to Parklands, we were moving to a social wasteland, reflecting a disgraceful lack of town planning insight, where these young people were left exposed to real mental and emotional poverty and trauma. There were no footpaths, no telephones, no shops, no bus system, no infrastructure at all.[62]

Christchurch is in danger of replicating this pattern again, with similar social consequences for its younger population.

Christchurch's centre has ruptured. To focus on the Anglican cathedral in the Square is to overlook the geographies of daily life. Will Cathedral Square be the heart of the city again? Despite the understandable shock and nostalgia, it appears that there is no stopping Christchurch's change of heart. The homage and last respects being paid to the cathedral indicate that, for better or for worse, the city is moving on.

BEYOND THE RUPTURE

A 2014 travel article for Air New Zealand's in-flight magazine *Kia Ora* was reminiscent of the 1952 Christchurch City Council promotional film (see Chapter 4). The article struggled to refocus its presentation of the city for visitors. Invoking the myths discussed in Chapter 2, it described how the city was '[o]nce famous for being "more English than the English"' and that it was 'created by hardy settlers, who cleared the plains and reclaimed the swamps'. It suggested: 'That pioneering spirit is evident once again in the city as a response to a series of rapid, drastic and painful changes that have occurred in the aftermath of the city's earthquakes.' But times had changed, and symbolic of the shift, 'A new breed of art is taking over where previously rows of old-fashioned planter beds were interspersed with traditional bronze statues of Queen Victoria and Sir Robert Falcon Scott.' The hegemonic landscapes reviewed in Chapter 1 were, more than ever, a part of the past.[1] Artist Tess Sheerin created three murals around the city in the wake of the earthquakes, 'Hope Bear' at the corner of Riccarton Road and Rotherham Street, 'Giraffing Around' in Liverpool Street off Hereford Street, and a mural on the Puaka/James Hight Library at the University of Canterbury. In an article in *Metropol* she commented: 'We have the potential to evolve into a unique, vibrant and creative city, and I feel that the unusual art projects that have emerged from such devastation are important for Christchurch to grow from.'[2]

Few Christchurch people foresaw such a devastating earthquake sequence. Popular myth held that Wellington was more likely to be hit. In hindsight, there were warning signs of what would happen in Christchurch in 2010 and 2011. In September 1988 Civil Defence officials modelled an 8.0 magnitude earthquake scenario for the city. This predicted that 'as many as 200 people' would be killed instantly, and that more than 4,000 would be seriously injured. In February 2011, 185 people lost their lives and 6,600 were seriously injured. Civil Defence also warned about the effects of liquefaction, and of substantial damage to Christchurch Hospital, which would struggle to remain operational. In 1996 geologist Mark Yetton shared the results from his three-year quake risk study; predictions included severe damage from land movement and liquefaction. Reflecting on these, an editorial in the *Press* in 2015 suggested that 'few people believed in the scenarios enough to actually do much about them'. The editorial added its own warning: the earlier studies suggested that the Alpine Fault would cause the earthquakes, rather than faults under Canterbury as happened in 2010 and 2011. Ominously, a rupture of the Alpine Fault remains overdue.

The Canterbury earthquakes have provided many lessons for the future, and Christchurch's response serves as a useful laboratory of rupture for other parts of New Zealand. The *Press* editorial was a plea for the whole country to learn from Canterbury's experience, and to support government legislation in the massive task of bringing New Zealand's at-risk buildings up to code. It warned the rest of the country not to take a miserly approach to raising building standards and stated, 'Heed the warnings now, and don't pretend it's 1988.' Cantabrians have been forced to leave the denial zone, and have developed 'earthquake eyes' that can spot dangerous buildings wherever they are: 'they look just like the unreinforced masonry buildings in Christchurch did before they collapsed or were pulled down,' the *Press* has observed.[3] In September 2015 Ann Brower, the sole survivor from a bus crushed by a building collapse on Colombo Street in February 2011, successfully urged the Parliamentary Select Committee on Building to shorten the time period for bringing earthquake-pronc buildings around New Zealand up to standard.[4] Forty people died in February 2011 because unreinforced masonry buildings collapsed.[5]

Recovering from and remembering the Canterbury earthquakes is complex and subject to constant change. The earthquakes have led to rapid reconstruction and re-imaginings of the city's past. Highlighting this change, a wide range of opinions have been aired in discussions about what form the public commemoration of Canterbury's earthquakes should take. For some a memorial should be aesthetic; for others utilitarian. Inspired by a feature in Munich constructed after the Second World War bombings, Donald Walker of Mount Pleasant suggested building a memorial hill from Christchurch's ruins.[6] In a competition for ideas for an official city memorial, organised by CERA, the six finalists were: a memorial wall with a reflective pond; a table and chairs; a green and peaceful landscape; walls and bird sounds evoking 'call and response'; a riverside promenade with a memorial wall; and a curved memorial wall.[7] The 150-metre marble curved wall, together with a riverside walkway and bridge to a small memorial garden, was selected and is currently under construction on Oxford Terrace between Montreal and Durham streets.

Missing from the public and official debate were the more significant forms of private and commercial remembrance already well under way. Since the September 2010 earthquake, Christchurch people have turned their city's past into many diverse souvenirs. These efforts reflect individual and private responses, but are also often commercial. Such tokens of 'earthquakery' bridge the division between public and private. They show that people do not wait for official, public memorials, but create their own cultures of history and remembrance. Why wait years for the Christ Church Cathedral to be rebuilt (or not) when you can immediately display it as a tattoo on your body? And perhaps you might ward off further disaster by draping a memory bead of a cracked house with a broken chimney around your wrist as a macabre lucky charm.

As part of the attempt to make sense of disaster, to remember and honour the dead, and to overcome and heal, the cult of earthquakery has thrived. In the aftermath of the quakes an ever-expanding range of jewellery, much of it featuring the Anglican and Catholic cathedrals, damaged houses, and numbers 7.1 and 6.3 on the Richter scale, was produced for sale. Prior to the earthquakes, Christchurch artisan business Beadz Unlimited was located in the Upstairs Galleria of the old Christchurch Boys' High School building in the Arts Centre on Worcester Boulevard. After the 2010 earthquake, it produced a special edition earthquake house charm, made in Christchurch by artisan jewellers, that was marketed as 'supporting local business'. Beadz Unlimited was able to pick up the pieces of its business and start afresh, and in August 2011 it opened a shop in St Albans.[8] Following its reinvention it produced a collection of jewelley featuring iconic Christchurch landmarks. New sterling silver and gold pieces were added, including the historic Worcester Boulevard building, an old tram, the Anglican cathedral, the Anglican cathedral's rose window, and lots of broken houses. Linking commerce to charity, one dollar from each sale went to the Christchurch Red Cross. All items continued to be 'made with love in Christchurch'.[9] By April 2011, Harding's Jewellers was selling a memory bead featuring the Anglican cathedral and two other memory beads with '6.3' and '7.1' on them.[10] They also produced an Anglican cathedral pendant and a rose window pendant. A Catholic cathedral pendant and a Catholic cathedral dome memory bead were later added to the collection.[11]

Following the trend begun during the Second World War in New Zealand, there were also calls for practical and socially useful memorials. But instead of the memorial halls and scholarships favoured in the past, individually useful items that raised money for Canterbury earthquake disaster relief proved incredibly popular. For example, down the road from Christchurch, the *Ashburton Guardian* reported that 'as mother nature socks it to Canterbury, Rural Women New Zealand has started producing some aftersocks of its own'. Justine and Jo Ottey approached the Ashburton Sock Company about the possibility of producing red and black socks (in Canterbury's provincial colours) featuring an earthquake shake line. They sold more than 1,500 pairs of their 'Aftersocks', priced at $20 each, in three days. In a short period 7,000 pairs had been sold. Profits went to the Christchurch Earthquake Mayoral Relief Fund.[12]

Back in Christchurch, a memento brick, the 'SILTY', was made from liquefaction silt collected from Hagley Park after the earthquake of 22 February 2011. Proceeds from the sales of the bricks went to the Greening the Rubble and Gap Filler organisations to assist in 'activating gaps in city streets created by the earthquakes' through temporary, creative and people-centred projects.[13] Such earthy urban reuse was part of a new post-quake city momentum explored in the publication *Once in a Lifetime: City Building after Disaster in Christchurch*.[14] Its pages resurrected the spirit of past garden city dreamers and communal visionaries. In a similar vein, garden historian Matt Morris advocated the development of an 'edible city' with community gardens and orchards on vacant sections and public land.[15]

Earthquakery was located in the post-quake Christchurch moment, but it also captured the past and reflected the mood of society. Sometimes it was humorous; at other times deadly serious. Earthquakery memorials borrowed and combined elements from the religious and secular, and from high and low culture. As memorials always have done, they fused images from the landscape using a range of media: gold, silver, cotton and wood. Road cones, 'one of Christchurch's most prolific post-quake symbols', were turned into ad hoc memorials. By the end of 2011, there were an estimated 40,000 to 60,000 road cones being used in the city. Christchurch Polytechnic Institute of Technology (CPIT) design students launched the 'Road Cone City' exhibition that featured transformed cones as a cake, an upturned ice cream, a gramophone horn, a snowy alp and quake scenes.[16] More kitsch commemoration was found in Christchurch chef Aaron Campbell's replica of Christ Church Cathedral's famed rose window using twenty-five kilograms of breakfast cereal stuck together with marshmallow, and covered with icing and acrylic paint.[17]

Significantly, most earthquakery was targeted at women. Women were among those who spoke out for alternative memorials through the twentieth century, and now, rather than donate their dollars to contribute to a grand public memorial, they chose to buy personally meaningful mini-memorials. Shattered heirloom crockery, for example, was fashioned into new treasures. Despite the masculinist tone of media accounts of heroic rescues, decision-makers' comments, and references to quake 'victims', the strong spirit of Canterbury's women as revealed in Chapter 3 lived on. It was evident in the Christchurch branch of the National Council of Women's 'Women's Voices' oral history project.[18] Led by sociologist Rosemary Du Plessis, the project recorded the everyday experiences of women during the quakes, traversing public and private spaces.

Along with the private and often bodily display of earthquakery, a simultaneous quiet public movement took place. Women's cultural pursuits assumed a constructive presence outside of the home. After the earthquakes women's art invaded public space, with knitting installations appearing at demolition sites. Another manifestation of women's material culture of care included impressive gifts of baking and intricate quilts.

With a percentage of the sale from earthquakery projects usually going towards earthquake relief, a social need was being addressed. There was the added benefit that local designers, artisans and businesses were being supported. The pervasive approach was to get on pragmatically with the rebuilding of Canterbury while memorialising what had happened. Earthquakery was brazen, unashamed, self-conscious; yet also charitable and often a form of quake commerce. Christchurch architectural designer Faye Pearson-Green, for example, produced a range of bags for the Christchurch Art Gallery Shop that was intended to both 'preserve our memories of the Christ Church Cathedral and carry our shopping in style'. She sketched the cathedral's rose window and made a screen print 'creating a lasting memory of the heart of our city'. The window featured on black calico tote bags, knee-highs, mugs, tea towels, T-shirts and umbrellas.[19]

Some fundraising was overtly religious. Shortly after the earthquakes, senior students at Cathedral Grammar School produced a five dollar commemorative earthquake badge, with proceeds from its sale going towards the rebuild of the Anglican cathedral.[20] Then Cathedral Grammar School teacher Clare Eramus and illustrator Vanessa Ide published two books (one about 'Kia Kaha the Cathedral mouse'), donating money from sales towards the redevelopment of the school and the cathedral.

Rebecca Lovell-Smith's 'Sure to Rise' tea towel captured the reality of the times, recalling the past and offering a pathway to the future. It featured a resurrected Christ Church Cathedral on an Edmonds Baking Powder tin, with the slogan 'Sure to Rise' and the words 'Christchurch, 22 February 2011, kia kaha and (munted)'. Ironically the heritage Edmonds building, with the 'Sure to Rise' slogan on its roof, had been demolished in 1989, yet it was evoked as if it were a part of the more immediate past.[21] 'Kia kaha' (stay strong) was a phrase used by the 28th Māori Battalion during the Second World War; the word 'munted' quickly became a byword for what had happened to Christchurch after it was first used by Mayor Bob Parker to describe the city. He said, 'It means totally destroyed, which suits what's going on around here.'[22]

The ruptures identified in this book indicate how the city might regroup and move on. Chapter 1, with its discussion of ruptured landscapes, warns of being ideologically trapped in the past. It suggests that too much of a colonial mindset can overshadow the importance of the local environment. What is good for other places will not necessarily suit a geologically volatile South Pacific earthquake zone. The rupturing of Christchurch has shown that being open to continual change is the best way forward.

The discussion of ruptured peoples and heritage in Chapter 2 suggests that respect for all peoples, regardless of race or ethnicity, and regardless of length of residency in the city, is the way to proceed. Just as cultural encounter was part of Christchurch's history, the earthquakes have provided the opportunity to break down barriers between diverse communities. It is time for dialogue. What place do settler formation narratives have in the post-quake city? How do such narratives fit with Ngāi Tahu's rapidly changing part in the city? How can all who live in the city be made to feel at home?

Chapter 3 indicates the possibility of learning from the strengths of the past. The Canterbury earthquakes have ruptured 'the People's Republic of Christchurch', bringing that radical heritage into question. Ironically, the alternative ways of living so prevalent in Christchurch's past have much to offer in the city's rebuild. There is scope for more bicycles, swimming pools, collectivism, peace advocacy and vigorous political discussion in a more caring, compassionate society. Where possible, it is time to make the most of Christchurch's discernible moderate streak and build bridges between so-called opposing 'left-wing' and 'conservative' factions.

Chapter 4 reveals that conformity and opposition to diversity is unproductive. Post-quake Christchurch has the chance to rise from a ruptured Gothic identity as a creative and inclusive place. It is clearly no longer the imagined 'English' place it used to be, in character, population or in the way it looks. Rather than remaining in denial and attempting to restore an Englishness that was always tenuous and restrictive, it is time to embrace the opportunity for a new postcolonial reality. Tourists can learn about the English garden city as history while experiencing contemporary innovation.

The rupture of the city's centre, discussed in Chapter 5, is deeply regrettable, yet it had its roots in market-led developments already under way before the earthquakes. Out of the tragic loss comes the opportunity for safety, sustainability and creativity. Recreation, commerce, tourism, and worship in the city's former centre would need much financial investment. It is time to think smaller in scale and not to attempt to restore what was there before the earthquakes. Cathedral Square will remain an evolving space and a work in progress, just as it always was. The proliferation of suburbs and xurbs is cause for concern and there is the risk of the emergence of a new 'suburban Gothic', consisting of carefully manicured properties in a social setting evocative of the mid-twentieth century.

Lovell-Smith's 'Sure to Rise' tea towel brought together diverse memories and symbols and printed them on a white cloth background in bright yellow and orange that glowed with the certainty of a sunny future and regenerated Cantabrian pride.

Christchurch would be a unique place situated in its own locale, yet mindful of global connectedness. The fallen past would live on in ways that people could only dare to imagine but that they could work to create. The past can help to make sense of the present. It reveals the twists, turns and complexities of landscape, hegemony and culture, and helps us to cope with disaster.

NOTES

The Rupture

1 Raphael Samuel, *Theatres of Memory: Past and Present in Contemporary Culture*, Verso, London and New York, 1994.

2 David Lowenthal, *The Past is a Foreign Country*, Cambridge University Press, Cambridge, 1985.

3 Kenneth Melvin, *New Zealand: The Small Utopia*, Collins, Auckland, 1962, p.125.

4 See Giselle Byrnes and Catharine Coleborne, 'Editorial Introduction: The Utility and Futility of "The Nation" in Histories of Aotearoa New Zealand', *New Zealand Journal of History*, 45, 1 (2011), pp.7–8. The value of comparative history that includes New Zealand is signalled in Graeme Wynn, 'Reflections on the Writing of New Zealand History', *New Zealand Journal of History*, 18, 2 (1984), pp.104–16.

5 Stephen Slemon, 'Unsettling the Empire: Resistance Theory for the Second World', in Padmini Mongia (ed.), *Postcolonial Theory: A Reader*, Arnold, London and New York, 1996, pp.72–83. For discussion of 'Better Britain' see James Belich, *Paradise Reforged: A History of the New Zealanders from the 1880s to the Year 2000*, Penguin/Allen Lane, Auckland, 2001.

6 See Dipesh Chakrabarty, *Provincializing Europe: Postcolonial Thought and Historical Difference*, Princeton University Press, Princeton and Oxford, 2000.

7 Eric Pawson, 'Postcolonial New Zealand?', in Kay Anderson and Faye Gayle (eds), *Cultural Geographies*, Longman, Melbourne, 1999, p.26.

8 See W. David McIntyre, *British Decolonization 1946–1987: When, Why and How Did the British Empire Fall?*, Macmillan/St Martin's Press, Basingstoke and New York, 1998.

9 Jane M. Jacobs, *Edge of Empire: Postcolonialism and the City*, Routledge, London and New York, 1996.

10 See James Duncan and David Ley (eds), *Place/Culture/Representation*, Routledge, London and New York, 2013; Audrey Kobayashi and

Suzanne Mackenzie (eds), *Remaking Human Geography*, Routledge, London and New York, 2014; Daniel Cosgrove and Stephen Daniels, *The Iconography of Landscape: Essays on the Symbolic Representation, Design and Use of Past Environments*, Cambridge University Press, Cambridge, 1988; and Donald Meinig and J. B. Jackson, *The Interpretation of Ordinary Landscapes: Geographical Essays*, Oxford University Press, Oxford, 1979.

11 See Andrew Hill Clark, *The Invasion of New Zealand by People, Plants and Animals: The South Island*, Rutgers University Press, New Brunswick, 1949; Kenneth B. Cumberland, *Landmarks*, Reader's Digest, Surry Hills, NSW, 1981. For an alternative view, see Eric Pawson, 'Confronting Nature', in John Cookson and Graeme Dunstall (eds), *Southern Capital: Christchurch: Towards a City Biography 1850–2000*, Canterbury University Press, Christchurch, 2000, pp.60–84.

12 Simon Schama, *Landscape and Memory*, Vintage Books, New York, 1995.

13 Fiona Farrell, *The Villa at the Edge of the Empire: One Hundred Ways to Read a City*, Penguin/Random House, Auckland, 2015.

14 Antonio Gramsci, 'Selections from the Prison Notebooks, X, "Intellectuals and Education"', in David Forgacs (ed.), *An Antonio Gramsci Reader: Selected Writings 1916–1935*, Schonken Books, New York, p.306; Raymond Williams, 'Selections from Marxism and Literature', in Nicholas B. Dirks and Sherry B. Ortner (eds), *Culture/Power/History: A Reader in Contemporary Social Theory*, Princeton University Press, Princeton, 1994, pp.598–99.

Chapter 1

1 Simon Schama, *Landscape and Memory*, Vintage, London and New York, 1995, p.9. For an example of 'spatial history', see Giselle Byrnes, *Boundary Markers: Land Surveying and the Colonisation of New Zealand*, Bridget Williams Books, Wellington, 2001.

2 Yi Fu Tuan, *Space and Place: The Perspective of Experience*, University of Minnesota Press, Minneapolis, 1977; Yi Fu Tuan, *Topophilia: A Study of Environmental Perception, Attitudes and Values*, Prentice Hall, Englewood Cliffs, N.J., 1974.

3 Charlie Gates, 'Broken Hearted', *Press*, 1 April 2011, p.8.

4 Mary Ann Steggles, 'Set in Stone: Victoria's Monuments in India', *History Today*, 51, 2 (2001).

5 'John Ballance statue', NZ Museums, www.nzmuseums.co.nz/account/4446/object/137177/John_Ballance (accessed 8 July 2015). See also Chris Maclean and Jock Phillips, *The Sorrow and the Pride: New Zealand War Memorials*, Historical Branch/GP Books, Wellington, 1990, pp.22–24.

6 For example, this happened in a 1987 Waitangi Day protest. See 'Sir George Grey statue, Auckland', Te Ara – The Encyclopedia of New Zealand, www.teara.govt.nz/en/photograph/32552/sir-george-grey-statue-auckland (accessed 8 July 2015).

7 Quake City: the Christchurch Earthquakes Story, www.canterburymuseum.com/quakecity/ (accessed 17 Sept 2014).

8 Gates, 'Broken Hearted'.

9 Jenny May, 'On the Move: The Godley Statue and the Godley Plot', in Mark Stocker (ed.), *Remembering Godley: a Portrait of Canterbury's Founder*, Hazard Press, Christchurch, 2001, pp.99–112.

10 Charles Cole, 'A Tale of Two Statues', *Press*, 15 February 2013, p.C4.

11 Patricia Burns, *Fatal Success: A History of the New Zealand Company*, Heinemann Reed, Auckland, 1989.

12 For details see chapters in Stocker, *Remembering Godley*.

13 'Settlers, Squatters and Surveyors: Shaping the Canterbury Settlement, 1848–1851', Archives New Zealand, http://archives.govt.nz/gallery/v/Online+Regional+Exhibitions/Chregionalofficegallery/sss/ (accessed 21 October 2015).

14 For an Australian example see Paul Carter, *The Road to Botany Bay: An Exploration in Landscape and History*, Faber & Faber, London, 1987.

15 W. David McIntyre, 'Outwards and Upwards – Building the City', in John Cookson and Graeme Dunstall (eds), *Southern Capital: Christchurch: Towards a City Biography, 1850–2000*, Canterbury University Press, Christchurch, 2000, pp.85–114.

16 *Peninsula and Plain: The History and Geography of*

Banks Peninsula and the Canterbury Plains, Whitcombe & Tombs, Christchurch, 1955 (revised edn 1974), p.59.

17 'Plate 55: Drains and Plagues', in Malcolm McKinnon, Barry Bradley and Russell Kirkpatrick (eds), *Bateman New Zealand Historical Atlas: Ko Papatuanuku e Takoto Nei*, David Bateman/Historical Branch, Department of Internal Affairs, Auckland, 1997.

18 J. P. Morrison, *The Evolution of a City*, Christchurch City Council, Christchurch, 1948, p.v.

19 G. A. Bremner, *Imperial Gothic: Religious Architecture and High Anglican Culture in the British Empire, c.1840–70*, Yale University Press, New Haven and London, 2013.

20 Bruce Ansley, *Christchurch Heritage: A Celebration of Lost Buildings and Streetscapes*, Random House, Auckland, 2011, back cover.

21 John Wilson, *Lost Christchurch*, Te Waihora Press, Lincoln, 1984.

22 'John Wilson', in Fiona Farrell and Juliet Nicholas, *The Quake Year*, Canterbury University Press, Christchurch, 2012, pp.195–205.

23 *Reconstruction: Conversations on a City*, Christchurch Art Gallery Te Puna o Waiwhetu, Christchurch, 2011.

24 See Ann Brower, 'Manifold Sins Cost 12 Lives', *Press*, 13 February 2012, www.stuff.co.nz/the-press/opinion/perspective/6406474/Manifold-sins-cost-12-lives (accessed 25 July 2015). Ann Brower was the sole survivor of thirteen people who were crushed by an unreinforced brick building at 603–613 Colombo Street on 22 February 2011. Nine people were on the No. 3 bus and four were on the footpath.

25 See Felicity Barnes, *New Zealand's London: A Colony and its Metropolis*, Auckland University Press, Auckland, 2012.

26 Shelley Robinson, 'Living through the London Blitz Compared to Quakes', *Star*, 7 February 2014, pp.2–3.

27 David Edgington, *Reconstructing Kobe: The Geography of Crisis and Opportunity*, UBC Press, Vancouver, 2010.

28 See Dipesh Chakravorty, *Provincialising Europe: Postcolonial Thought and Historical Difference*,

Princeton University Press, Princeton and Oxford, 2000.

29 Perry T. Royal, 'Home Architects', *Metropol*, 4 August 2011, p.43.

30 Martin van Beynen, 'One year on too soon to shake raw feelings', *Press*, 18 February 2012, p.C10.

Chapter 2

1 '2013 Census QuickStats about Greater Christchurch', Statistics New Zealand, www.stats.govt.nz/Census/2013-census/profile-and-summary-reports/quickstats-about-greater-chch (accessed 27 February 2015).

2 Ibid.

3 Kurt Bayer, 'Boom time for sex industry. Rebuild brings influx of prostitutes to city', *Star*, 20 January 2012, p.1.

4 Jack Montgomerie, 'Foreign Workers Flock to Christchurch Rebuild', *Critic*, 17 (2013), www.critic.co.nz/news/article/3152/foreign-workers-flock-to-christchurch-rebuild (accessed 27 February 2015).

5 Ibid.

6 Ibid.

7 '2013 Census QuickStats about Greater Christchurch', Statistics New Zealand, www.stats.govt.nz/Census/2013-census/profile-and-summary-reports/quickstats-about-greater-chch (accessed 27 February 2015).

8 Montgomerie, 'Foreign Workers Flock to Christchurch Rebuild'.

9 Tess McClure, 'Migrants "Treated Like Bonded Labour"', *Press*, 26 August 2014, www.stuff.co.nz/the-press/news/10422562/ (accessed 27 February 2015).

10 Gwenda Turner, *Christchurch: An Enchanted Journey through the Garden City*, Penguin, Auckland, 1999, p.7.

11 Megan Woods, 'Integrating the Nation: Gendering Maori Urbanization and Integration 1942–1969', PhD thesis, University of Canterbury, 2002, p.62.

12 Geoffrey Rice, *Lyttelton: Port and Town*, Canterbury University Press, Christchurch, 2004, p.14; Melanie Riwai-Couch, *Ngai Tahu Battles*, M. Riwai-Couch, Christchurch, 2008.

13 Te Maire Tau, 'Ngāi Tahu', Te Ara – the Encyclopedia of New Zealand, www.TeAra.govt.nz/en/ngai-tahu (accessed 13 June 2015).

14 Ibid.

15 Atholl Anderson, Judith

Binney and Aroha Harris, *Tangata Whenua: An Illustrated History*, Bridget Williams Books, Wellington, 2014, p.185.

16 John Deans (with G. M. Miller), *Pioneers on Port Cooper Plains: The Deans Family of Riccarton and Homebush*, Simpson and Williams, Christchurch, 1964, pp.28, 31.

17 Gordon Ogilvie, *Pioneers of the Plains: The Deans of Canterbury*, Shoal Bay Press, Christchurch, 1996, p.38.

18 'Homebush – "The home of Canterbury's founding Deans family" ruined', *Press*, 6 September 2010, p.1.

19 Te Maire Tau and Atholl Anderson (eds), *Ngāi Tahu: A Migration History: The Carrington Text*, Bridget Williams Books/Te Rūnanga O Ngāi Tahu, Wellington and Christchurch, 2008, p.201.

20 Geoffrey W. Rice, *Victoria Square: Cradle of Christchurch*, Canterbury University Press, Christchurch, 2014, p.16.

21 Vincent O'Malley, *Beyond the Imperial Frontier: The Contest for Colonial New Zealand*, Bridget Williams Books, Wellington, 2014, pp.54–55.

22 Peter Maling, *The Torlesse Papers: The Journals and Letters of Charles Obins Torlesse Concerning the Foundation of the Canterbury Settlement in New Zealand, Christchurch*, Caxton Press, Christchurch, 2003, p.103.

23 Tau and Anderson (eds), *Ngai Tahu*, p.201.

24 Ibid., pp.201–2.

25 Te Marie Tau, 'Ngai Tahu – From "Better Dead and Out of the Way" to "To Be Seen to Belong"', in John Cookson and Graeme Dunstall (eds), *Southern Capital: Christchurch: Towards a City Biography, 1850–2000*, Canterbury University Press, Christchurch, 2000, p.223.

26 Ogilvie, *Pioneers of the Plains*, p.7. They arrived with the Manson and Gebbie families.

27 Colin Amodeo (with Ron Chapman), *Forgotten Forty-Niners, Being an Account of the Men and Women Who Paved the Way in 1849 for the Canterbury Pilgrims in 1850*, Caxton Press, Christchurch, 2003, p.176; 'Wairau affray, 1843', Te Ara – the Encyclopedia of New Zealand, www.teara.govt.nz/en/artwork/28561/wairau-affray-1843 (accessed 21 October 2015).

28 Ogilvie, *Pioneers of the Plains*, p.11.
29 Ibid., p.32.
30 Deans, *Pioneers on Port Cooper Plains*, p.29.
31 Harry C. Evison, *Te Wai Pounamu: The Greenstone Island: A History of the Southern Maori During the European Colonization of New Zealand*, Aoraki Press, Wellington and Christchurch, 1993, p.214.
32 Ibid., pp.214–15.
33 Deans, *Pioneers on Port Cooper Plains*, p.24.
34 Jane Deans, *Letters to my Grandchildren*, 3rd edn, Cadsonbury Publications, Christchurch, 1995, p.27.
35 Tipene O'Regan, 'Ngai Tahu and the Crown: Partnership Promised', in Garth Cant and Russell Kirkpatrick (eds), *Rural Canterbury: Celebrating its History*, Daphne Brasell Associates Limited, Lincoln University Press and Whitireia Publishing, Lincoln, 2001, p.18.
36 Deans, *Letters to my Grandchildren*, p.7.
37 O'Malley, *Beyond the Imperial Frontier*, p.199.
38 Deans, *Letters to my Grandchildren*, pp.9, 7.
39 Ibid., p.75.
40 Colin Amodeo, *The Summer Ships, Being an Account of the First Six Ships Sent Out from England to New Zealand by the Canterbury Association in 1850–1851*, Caxton Press, Christchurch, 2000, pp.17, 304; *The First Four Ships: Canterbury Colonist Families Share their Histories*, *Press*, Christchurch, October 2006.
41 Rice, *Victoria Square*, p.21.
42 Amodeo, *The Summer Ships*, p.11.
43 Amodeo, *Forgotten Forty-Niners*, p.vii.
44 Amodeo, *Forgotten Forty-Niners*, p.vii, and Amodeo, *Summer Ships*, p.305.
45 Amodeo, *Forgotten Forty-Niners*, p.180.
46 Rice, *Victoria Square*, p.39.
47 Ibid., p.40.
48 Atholl Anderson, *The Welcome of Strangers*, Otago University Press, Dunedin, 1998, pp.129–30.
49 Rice, *Victoria Square*, p.151.
50 Rice, *Victoria Square*, p.264; *Press*, 4 April 1995, p.3.
51 Ann Parsonson, 'Ngai Tahu – The Whale That Awoke – From Claim to Settlement (1960–1998)', in Cookson and Dunstall (eds), *Southern Capital*, p.251.

52 Woods, 'Integrating the Nation', p.29.

53 Angela Wanhalla, *In/Visible Site: the Mixed-Descent Families of Southern New Zealand*, Bridget Williams Books, Wellington, 2009, p.4.

54 Quoted in Roger Duff, 'South Island Maoris', in L.L.G. Sutherland (ed.), *The Maori People Today: A General Survey*, New Zealand Institute of International Affairs and the New Zealand Council for Educational Research, Wellington, 1940, p.386.

55 Woods, 'Integrating the Nation', p.28.

56 Tau, 'Ngai Tahu', in *Southern Capital*, pp.236–41.

57 Ibid., p.241.

58 Ibid., pp.228–31.

59 Anderson, Binney and Harris, *Tangata Whenua*, p.466.

60 Ibid., p.468.

61 Ibid., p.469.

62 Tau and Anderson, *Ngai Tahu*, p.205.

63 Draft Central City Plan, Summary Document, August 2011, CERA, Te Rūnanga o Ngāi Tahu and Environment Canterbury, p.4.

64 Simon Lambert, 'Impacts on Māori of the Ōtautahi/ Christchurch Earthquakes', Te Whanake, Faculty of Environment, Society, and Design Working Paper 2013-01, Lincoln University, 2013, pp.7–10.

65 '2013 Census QuickStats about Greater Christchurch', Statistics New Zealand, www.stats.govt.nz/Census/2013-census/profile-and-summary-reports/qstats-greater-chch-mr.aspx (accessed 10 June 2015).

66 E. Tarena, 'He Toki Ki Te Rika – Revitalising Maori Trade Training', paper presented at the International Indigenous Development Research Conference, Auckland, 2012.

67 Gerard Smyth, *When a City Falls*, Frank Film, 2011.

68 Mark Whyte, Susan Wakefield, Local Heroes Trust, *Twelve Local Heroes: A Celebration: A Set of Bronze Busts Commissioned by the Local Heroes Trust*, Local Heroes Trust, Christchurch, 2009, p.3.

69 'Canterbury Heroes', Christchurch City Libraries, http://christchurchcitylibraries.com/society/people/canterbury-heroes/Canterbury Heroes (accessed 12 March 2015).

70 Sarona Meata'a Aiono-Iosefa, 'Shifting Sands', in

Peggy Fairbairn Dunlop and Gabrielle Makisi (eds), *Making Our Place: Growing Up PI in New Zealand*, Dunmore Press, Palmerston North, 2003, p.102.

71 Jonathan Mane-Wheoki, 'The High Arts in a Regional Culture – from Englishness to Self-Reliance', in Cookson and Dunstall (eds), *Southern Capital*, pp.323–24.

72 Sean Mallon, Kolokesa Mahina-Tuai and Damon Salesa (eds), *Tangata o le Moana: New Zealand and the People of the Pacific*, Te Papa Press, Wellington, 2012, p.323.

73 Ibid., p.322.

74 Kobayashi, Audrey, '"Here we go again": Christchurch's Anti-racism Rally as a Discursive Crisis', in Julie Cupples (ed.), *New Zealand Geographer* special issue, 65 (2009), pp.60, 70.

75 Carl Davidson, 'Stopping the Racist Jerk in a Crowd', *Press*, 3 September 2015, p.A11.

Chapter 3

1 Jim McAloon, 'Radical Christchurch', in John Cookson and Graeme Dunstall (eds), *Southern Capital: Christchurch: Towards a City Biography, 1850–2000*, Christchurch, Canterbury University Press, 2000, pp.162–92.

2 Kay Douglas, *Life Out Loud: 22 Inspiring New Zealand Women Share Their Wisdom*, HarperCollins, Auckland, 2001, p.80.

3 Ibid., pp.80, 83.

4 'People's Republic Targets Brewer', *Press*, 1 May 1988, p.7.

5 McAloon, 'Radical Christchurch', p.191.

6 W. David McIntyre, 'FitzGerald, James Edward', from *The Dictionary of New Zealand Biography*, Te Ara – the Encyclopedia of New Zealand, www.TeAra.govt.nz/en/biographies/1f9/fitzgerald-james-edward (accessed 13 November 2015).

7 Edmund Bohan, *Blest Madman: FitzGerald of Canterbury*, Canterbury University Press, Christchurch, 1998.

8 McIntyre, 'FitzGerald, James Edward'.

9 Keith Sinclair, *William Pember Reeves*, Reed, Auckland, 1969, pp.19–21.

10 P. G. McHugh, 'William Pember Reeves (1857–1932): Lawyer, Politician, Journalist, Statesman, Poet, Historian, and "Rough Architect" of the New Zealand State', in

Shaunnagh Dorsett and Ian Hunter (eds), *Law and Politics in British Colonial Thought: Transpositions of Empire*, Palgrave, Basingstoke and New York, 2010, pp.187–205.

11 Sinclair, *William Pember Reeves*, pp.18, 26.

12 McAloon, 'Radical Christchurch', p.162.

13 McHugh, 'William Pember Reeves', p.187.

14 Ibid., pp.189, 193.

15 Sinclair, *William Pember Reeves*, p.6.

16 Charlotte Macdonald, 'Kate Sheppard', in Charlotte Macdonald, Merimeri Penfold and Bridget Williams (eds), *The Book of New Zealand Women: Ko Kui Ma Te Kaupapa*, Bridget Williams Books, Wellington, 1991, pp.604–7.

17 Margaret Lovell-Smith, *Plain Living, High Thinking: The Family Story of Jennie and Will Lovell-Smith, A History of the Lovell-Smith Family*, Pedmore Press, Christchurch, 1995.

18 W. J. Gardner, 'Hall, John', from *The Dictionary of New Zealand Biography*, Te Ara – the Encyclopedia of New Zealand, www.TeAra.govt.nz/en/biographies/1h5/hall-john (accessed 17 June 2015).

19 Jean Garner, *By His Own Merits: Sir John Hall: Pioneer, Pastoralist and Premier*, Dryden Press, Christchurch, 1995.

20 Tessa K. Malcolm, 'Sheppard, Katherine Wilson', in *The Suffragists: Women Who Worked for the Vote*, Bridget Williams Books/ Dictionary of New Zealand Biography, Wellington, 1993, p.122.

21 Clare Simpson, 'A Social History of Women and Cycling in Late Nineteenth Century New Zealand', PhD thesis, Lincoln University, 1998, p.11.

22 Ibid., p.162.

23 Sandra Coney (ed.), *Standing in the Sunshine: A History of New Zealand Women Since They Won the Vote*, Penguin Viking, Auckland, 1993, p.113.

24 McAloon, 'Radical Christchurch', p.171.

25 Ibid., p.172.

26 Margaret Lovell-Smith, *Easily the Best, The Life of Helen Connon 1857–1903*, Canterbury University Press, Christchurch, 2004, p.117.

27 Ibid., p.7.

28 Ibid., p.117.

29 See *The Memoirs of Millicent Baxter*, Cape Catley, Whatamongo Bay, Queen Charlotte Sound, 1981.

30 Karen Fox and Katie Pickles, 'Success in Their Own Right: Dames on Top of the New Zealand Royal Honours System, 1917–2000', *History Now*, 11, 1 and 2 (2005), pp.24–30.

31 See Ian Dougherty, *The People's University: A Centennial History of the Canterbury Workers' Educational Association 1915–2015*, Canterbury University Press, Christchurch, 2015.

32 William Metcalf, 'Federative Home', in *Communal Societies*, 24 (2004), pp.26, 27.

33 'Report of the Special Committee of Enquiry into the Department of Chemistry and Physics, The Special Committee's Report', Canterbury College, Christchurch, 23 February 1895, p.1.

34 Ibid., p.73.

35 Ibid., p.5.

36 Ibid., p.73.

37 Ibid., p.77.

38 Metcalf, 'Federative Home', p.25.

39 McAloon, 'Radical Christchurch', p.173.

40 Lucy Sargisson and Lyman Tower-Sargent, *Living in Utopia – New Zealand's Intentional Communities*, Ashgate, Aldershot, 2004, pp.21, 25.

41 Tim Baker, *Professor Bickerton's Wainoni*, T. D. Baker, Christchurch, 2004, pp.66, 26.

42 Brittany Mann, 'Cyclist Fined For Blocking Hill Traffic', *Press*, 18 June, p.A1.

43 Baker, *Professor Bickerton's Wainoni*, p.1.

44 Metcalf, 'Federative Home', p.31.

45 Ibid., pp.24–32.

46 Ibid., pp.26–34.

47 Ibid., p.40.

48 Glyn Strange, *The Arts Centre of Christchurch: Then and Now*, Clerestory Press, Christchurch, 1994, p.13.

49 *The Weekly Press*, 18 March 1908, p.48, in Baker, *Professor Bickerton's Wainoni*, p.43.

50 Baker, *Professor Bickerton's Wainoni*, pp.33, 46–48.

51 Jane Tolerton, *Ettie: A Life of Ettie Rout*, Penguin, Auckland, 1992, p.241.

52 'Chippenham Lodge', Heritage New Zealand, www.heritage.org.nz/the-list/details/1846 (accessed 3 July 2015).

53 Sargisson and Tower-Sargent, *Living in Utopia*, p.84.

54 Ibid., p.87.

55 Charlie Gates, 'Hidden St Albans Jewel to be Restored', *Press*, 20 October 2012, www.stuff.co.nz/the-press/news/christchurch-earthquake-2011/7841995/Hidden-St-Albans-jewel-to-be-restored (accessed 3 July 2015); Lois Cairns, 'Historic Home Just too Good to Hide, *Press*, 14 May 2014, www.stuff.co.nz/the-press/news/10041096/Historic-home-just-too-good-to-hide (accessed 3 July 2015).

56 Stevan Eldred Grigg, *A New History of Canterbury*, John McIndoe, Dunedin, 1982, p.222.

57 McAloon, 'Radical Christchurch', p.162.

58 Tolerton, *Ettie*, pp.227–41.

59 Ibid., p.19

60 See Elizabeth Mathews, *Cora: A Wilding Seed*, Inyx Books, Cheviot, 1999.

61 Eric Pawson, 'Ell, Henry George', from *The Dictionary of New Zealand Biography*, Te Ara – the Encyclopedia of New Zealand, www.TeAra.govt.nz/en/biographies/3e4/ell-henry-george (accessed 4 June 2015).

62 Peter Graham, *So Brilliantly Clever: Parker, Hulme and the Murder that Shocked the World*, Awa Press, Wellington, 2011, p.57.

63 Glyn Strange, *The Little Theatre: Golden Years of the New Zealand Stage*, Clerestory Press, Christchurch, 2000.

64 Joanne Drayton, *Rhona Haszard: An Experimental Expatriate New Zealand Artist*, Canterbury University Press and UNITEC, Christchurch, 2002.

65 Jonathan Mane-Wheoki, 'The High Arts in a Regional Culture – from Englishness to Self-Reliance', in Cookson and Dunstall, *Southern Capital*, p.299.

66 Jim Anderton, *Heroes: Portraits of Inspiring New Zealanders*, Random House, Auckland, 1999, p.110.

67 Ibid., pp.115–16.

68 Ibid., p.110.

69 Michael Bassett, 'Kirk, Norman Eric', from *The Dictionary of New Zealand Biography*, Te Ara – the Encyclopedia of New Zealand, www.TeAra.govt.nz/en/biographies/5k12/kirk-norman-eric (accessed 10 July 2015).

70 James Belich, *Paradise Reforged: A History of the New Zealanders from the 1880s to the Year 2000*, Allen Lane/

Penguin, Auckland, 2001, p.399.

71 McAloon, 'Radical Christchurch', p.191.

72 Simon Collins, 'People's Republic flies National's blue banner', *New Zealand Herald,* 28 November 2011, www.nzherald.co.nz/nz/news/article.cfm?c_id=1&objectid=10769242, (accessed 23 January 2016).

73 Nicole Mathewson, Georgina Stylianou and Tim Fulton, 'Election: Canterbury Decides', *Press,* 20 September 2014, www.stuff.co.nz/the-press/news/10524525/Election-2014-Canterbury-decides (accessed 7 March 2015).

74 Simon Collins, 'People's Republic flies National's blue banner'.

75 Mathewson, Stylianou and Fulton, 'Election: Canterbury Decides'.

76 Consultation document, Christchurch City Council, March–April 1915.

77 Geoffrey W. Rice, *Christchurch Changing,* Canterbury University Press, Christchurch, 2000, p.146.

78 Maire Leadbeater, *Peace, Power and Politics: How New Zealand Became Nuclear Free,* Otago University Press, Dunedin, 2013, p.9.

79 Elsie Locke, *Peace People: A History of Peace Activities in New Zealand,* Hazard Press, Christchurch and Melbourne, 1992, p.253.

80 Ibid., pp.262–66.

81 Ibid., p.262.

82 Leadbeater, *Peace, Power and Politics,* pp.16–17.

83 Katie Pickles, 'Southern Outreach: New Zealand Claims Antarctica from the "Heroic Era" to the Twenty-first Century', in Katie Pickles and Catharine Coleborne (eds), *New Zealand's Empire,* Manchester University Press, Manchester and New York, 2015, pp. 229–44.

84 Leadbeater, *Peace, Power and Politics,* pp.70–71, p.83.

85 Ibid., p.257.

86 Editorial, *Race, Gender, Class,* 1, 1 (July 1985), p.1.

87 *Western News,* 28 April 2014, p.1.

88 *Press,* 3 November 2011, p.A14.

89 Andrew King and Gabrielle Stuart, 'Buck Blasts Voter Revolt Call', 8 July 2015, *Star,* p.1.

90 John Cookson, 'Towards a City Biography', in Cookson and Dunstall (eds), *Southern Capital,* pp.353–63.

Chapter 4

1 John MacKenzie, *Orientalism: History, Theory and the Arts*, Manchester University Press, Manchester and New York, 1995.

2 Stephen Murray, *Plotting Gothic*, Chicago University Press, Chicago and London, 2014.

3 See Cynthia Sugars, *Canadian Gothic: Literature, History, and the Spectre of Self-Invention*, University of Wales Press, Cardiff, 2014; Jacqueline Z. Wilson, 'Gothic: The Medieval Legacy in Australian Dark Tourism', in *Prison: Cultural Memory and Dark Tourism*, Peter Lang Publishing, New York, 2008, pp.31–50.

4 Misha Kavka, Jennifer Lawn and Mary Paul (eds), *Gothic New Zealand: The Darker Side of Kiwi Culture*, Otago University Press, Dunedin, 2006.

5 Ian J. Lochhead, *A Dream of Spires: Benjamin Mountfort and the Gothic Revival*, Canterbury University Press, Christchurch, 1999.

6 Howard McNaughton, 'Reinscribing the Urban Abject: Ngai Tahu and the Gothic Revival', *New Zealand Geographer*, 65, 1 (2009), pp.48–58.

7 'Sunnyside Hospital', Christchurch City Libraries, http://my.christchurchcitylibraries.com/sunnyside-hospital/ (accessed 22 May 2015).

8 McNaughton, 'Reinscribing the Urban Abject', p.48.

9 James Belich and Lydia Wevers with Richard Hill and Brigitte Bonisch-Brednich, 'Understanding New Zealand Cultural Identities', Discussion paper prepared by the Stout Research Centre for New Zealand Studies, Victoria University of Wellington, for the Ministry for Culture and Heritage, 2008, p.9.

10 *Cinema of Unease: a Personal Journey by Sam Neill*, BFI TV, NZ Film Commission, NZ On Air, TV3 Network Services in association with Top Shelf Productions, 1995.

11 Brenda Allen, 'Cinema of Unease', in James E. Bennett and Rebecca Beirne, *Making Film and Television Histories: Australia and New Zealand*, I.B. Tauris, London and New York, 2012, p.111.

12 Thelma Strongman, *City Beautiful: The First 100 Years of the Christchurch Beautifying Association*, Clerestory Press, Christchurch, 1999, pp.5, 10, 16.

13 Ibid., p.vii.

14 'Christchurch – Garden City of New Zealand', NZ On Screen, www.nzonscreen.com/title/christchurch-garden-city-of-new-zealand-1952 (accessed 10 April 2015).

15 Catherine Hall, *White, Male and Middle Class: Explorations in Feminism and History*, Routledge, London and New York, 1992, p.26.

16 Marjory Harper, '"Everything is English": Expectations, Experiences and Impacts of English Migrants to New Zealand, 1840–1970', in Lyndon Fraser and Angela McCarthy, *Far From Home: The English in New Zealand*, Otago University Press, Dunedin, 2012, p.39.

17 Jim McAloon, 'The Christchurch Elite', in John Cookson and Graeme Dunstall (eds), *Southern Capital: Christchurch: Towards a City Biography, 1850–2000*, Canterbury University Press, Christchurch, 2000, pp.193–221.

18 David Hackett Fischer, *Fairness and Freedom: A History of Two Open Societies: New Zealand and the United States*, Oxford University Press, New York, 2012, p.xiv.

19 Lyndon Fraser, *To Tara via Holyhead: Irish Catholic Immigrants in Nineteenth-Century Christchurch*, Auckland University Press, Auckland, 1997, p.51.

20 Ibid., p.61.

21 Stevan Eldred Grigg, *A New History of Canterbury*, John McIndoe, Dunedin, 1982, p.20.

22 John Cookson, 'Pilgrim's Progress – Image, Identity and Myth', in Cookson and Dunstall (eds), *Southern Capital*, p.28.

23 Redmer Yska, 'Dutch', Te Ara – the Encyclopedia of New Zealand, www.TeAra.govt.nz/en/dutch/page-2 (accessed 14 May 2015).

24 James E. Bennett, 'Heavenly Creatures: The 1954 Parker-Hulme Case', in Bennett and Beirne, *Making Film and Television Histories*, p.201.

25 Ibid., p.200.

26 Peter Graham, *So Brilliantly Clever: Parker, Hulme and the Murder That Shocked the World*, Awa Press, Wellington, 2011, p.20.

27 Bennett, 'Heavenly Creatures', p.199.

28 Rebecca Macfie, 'Bipolar Creatures?', *New Zealand Listener*, 19–25 November 2011, pp. 24–27.

29 Graham, *So Brilliantly Clever*, p.3.

30 Ibid., p.2.

31 Alison Laurie and Julie Glamuzina, *Parker and Hulme: A Lesbian View*, New Women's Press, Auckland, 1991, pp.28–35.

32 Graham, *So Brilliantly Clever*, p.66.

33 Ibid., pp.55–57.

34 Ibid., n.p. [photo insert caption].

35 Joanne Drayton, *The Search for Anne Perry*, HarperCollins, Auckland, 2012, p.255.

36 Ibid., pp.288, 280.

37 'Ballantyne's Fire', Christchurch City Libraries, http://my.christchurchcitylibraries.com/ballantynes-fire/ (accessed 24 January 2016).

38 *Star*, 19 November 2014, pp.1–3. A stonemason donated his time to repair the memorial and a $71,000 lotteries grant and donations from families of the victims helped to pay for the memorial rebuild and restoration.

39 Redmer Yska, *All Shook Up: The Flash Bodgie and the Rise of the New Zealand Teenager in the Fifties*, Penguin, Auckland, 1993; Chris Brickell, 'Sexuality, Morality and Society', in Giselle Byrnes (ed.), *New Oxford History of New Zealand*, Oxford University Press, Melbourne, 2009, p.474.

40 Graham, *So Brilliantly Clever*, p.173.

41 Laurie and Glamuzina, *Parker and Hulme*, p.18.

42 Drayton, *The Search for Anne Perry*, p.204.

43 Graham, *So Brilliantly Clever*, pp.30, 31; Laurie and Glamuzina, *Parker and Hulme*, pp.38–39.

44 St Margaret's College Archives, St Margaret's College Admission Book, Vol. 3, 1946–1963 [Archives Reference: SMC 121-168d].

45 Bill Pearson, 'Fretful Sleepers: A Sketch of New Zealand Behaviour and its Implications for the Artist', *Landfall: A New Zealand Quarterly*, September 1952, pp.201–30; Paul Millar, *No Fretful Sleeper: A Life of Bill Pearson*, Auckland University Press, Auckland, 2010.

46 Graham, *So Brilliantly Clever*, p.278.

47 Laurie and Glamuzina, *Parker and Hulme*, p.35.

48 Nadia Gush, 'Fraternal Fracture and the Court of Law: New Zealand's 1954

Parker–Hulme Trial', *Law and Literature*, 26, 3 (2014), pp.303–319.

49 Chris Brickell, *Southern Men: Gay Lives in Pictures*, Genre Press, Dunedin, 2014, p.11.

50 Ibid., p.117.

51 Tony Simpson, 'So Far To Go: Law Reform Has Been Driven by Less Noble Factors Than a Thirst for Justice', *New Zealand Listener*, 15 March 2014, pp.21–23.

52 Maureen Molloy, 'Death and the Maiden: The Feminine and the Nation in Recent New Zealand Films', *Signs: Journal of Women in Culture and Society*, 25, 1 (1999), pp.153–70.

53 Drayton, *The Search for Anne Perry*, p.327. Drayton has also written about Dame Ngaio Marsh, another famous crime writer with a strong Christchurch association.

54 Lynley Hood, *A City Possessed: The Civic Creche Case: Child Abuse, Gender Politics and the Law*, Longacre Press, Dunedin, 2001; Bronwyn Dalley, 'Child Abuse', Te Ara – the Encyclopedia of New Zealand, www.TeAra.govt.nz/en/video/30538/christchurch-civic-creche (accessed 24 May 2015).

Chapter 5

1 *Avenues*, June 2011, back cover.

2 *Mainland Press*, 9 November 2011, p.2.

3 See Trevor Burnard, 'An Artisanal Town – The Economic Sinews of Christchurch', in John Cookson and Graeme Dunstall (eds), *Southern Capital: Christchurch: Towards a City Biography, 1850–2000*, Canterbury University Press, Christchurch, 2000, pp.115–37.

4 *Star*, 11 June 2014, www.christchurchstar.co.nz (accessed 26 May 2015).

5 *Sunday Star Times*, 22 May 2011, p.A7.

6 Ian Lochhead, 'Connections to the Past Run Deep', *Press*, 6 October 2014, p.A11.

7 *Press*, 14 January 2012, p.A20.

8 *Press*, 'Cathedral Future Now Uncertain', 16 June 2011, p.A1.

9 *Press*, 17 June, 2011, p.A18.

10 *Press*, 15 June, 2011, p.D4.

11 *Mainland Press*, 18 May 2011, p.15.

12 'Chalice', Christchurch City Council, www.ccc.govt.nz/culture-and-community/heritage/heritage-in-the-city/chalice/ (accessed 20 July 2015).

13 *Press*, 19 November 2011, p.A3.
14 *Aftermath Heritage Matters*, Paua Productions, 2013.
15 'Editorial: The Price of Heritage', *Press*, 28 September 2011, www.stuff.co.nz/the-press/opinion/5694123/Editorial-The-price-of-heritage (accessed 13 November 2015).
16 *Press*, 11 November, 2011, p.A18.
17 *Press*, 10 November, 2011, p.A1.
18 *Press*, 9 November 2011, p.A18.
19 *Press*, 3 November 2011, p.A14.
20 *Press*, 5 November 2011, p.A23.
21 *Press*, editorial, 11 November 2011, p.A18.
22 *Press*, 10 November 2011, p.A16.
23 'Past Elections', Christchurch City Council, www.ccc.govt.nz/the-council/how-the-council-works/council-elections/past-elections/ (accessed 20 July 2015).
24 'No Strife with Dean – Bishop', *Press*, 13 December 2011, p.A3.
25 *Press*, 'A Statement from the Anglican Bishop of Christchurch about Christ Church Cathedral', 18 February 2012, p.C10.
26 Marc Greenhill, *Press*, 1 April 2011, p.A7.
27 Undated newspaper clipping.
28 Great Christchurch Buildings Trust, www.amazingcathedral.co.nz/portals/315/images/pressarticle.pdf (accessed 10 June 2015).
29 'Cathedral Demolition Ruling Upheld', Radio New Zealand News, www.radionz.co.nz/news/national/215434/cathedral-demolition-ruling-upheld (accessed 10 June 2015).
30 'RALLY FOR THE CATHEDRAL – SAVE OUR HERITAGE!', *Press*, 24 May 2012, p.B3; Great Christchurch Buildings Trust, www.amazingcathedral.co.nz (accessed 10 June 2015).
31 'Final Cathedral Designs Options Unveiled', *Press*, 4 April 2013, www.stuff.co.nz/the-press/business/the-rebuild/8504585/Final-Cathedral-design-options-unveiled 4/4/13 (accessed 10 June 2015).
32 Transitional Cathedral, Christchurch, New Zealand, www.cardboardcathedral.org.nz/ (accessed 10 June 2015).
33 Marc Greenhill, *Press*, 1 April 2011, p.A7.
34 'Sir Miles Warren Design May Break Four-Year Christ Church Cathedral Deadlock', *Press*, 18 March

2015, www.stuff.co.nz/the-press/business/the-rebuild/67428956/Sir-Miles-Warren-design-may-break-four-year-Christ-Church-Cathedral-deadlock (accessed 10 June 2015).

35 Peter Bluck, *Once and Future Cathedral,* Bluck's Books/ On Demand Printing, n.d., p.1

36 Ibid., pp.1–2, 6–7.

37 *Press,* 3 June, 2015, p.A16.

38 *Press,* 27 March 2015, p.A15.

39 Bob Parker and Tony Farrington, *Ripped Apart: A City in Chaos: Bob Parker's Story,* Antares Publishing, Kerikeri, 2012, pp.146–47.

40 *Press,* 7 November 2011, p.A14.

41 'Pause by the Ruins Then Step Boldly', *Press,* 9 August 2012, www.stuff.co.nz/the-press/opinion/perspective/5411813/Pause-by-the-ruins-then-step-boldly (accessed 14 November 2015).

42 *Star,* 11 March 2015, p.3.

43 Federation of University Women, *Round the Square,* Clerestory Press, Christchurch, 1995.

44 David Cook, *Meet Me in the Square: Christchurch 1983–1987,* Christchurch Art Gallery, Christchurch, 2014.

45 Redmer Yska, 'Meet Me in the Square', *Bulletin,* 178 (Summer, December 2014–February 2015), Christchurch Art Gallery, pp.23–29.

46 '2013 Census QuickStats about Greater Christchurch', Statistics New Zealand, www.stats.govt.nz/Census/2013-census/profile-and-summary-reports/quickstats-about-greater-chch (accessed 4 March 2015).

47 Ibid.

48 Ibid.

49 Tom Doudney, 'Post-quake Traffic Shifts to Outskirts', *Star,* 11 March 2015, p.7.

50 Peter Perry, 'A Geography of Governance', in Cookson and Dunstall (eds), *Southern Capital,* p. 279.

51 Bruce Ansley, *Gods and Little Fishes: A Boy and a Beach,* Longacre Press, Dunedin, 2009.

52 Yi Fu Tuan, *Topophilia: A Study of Environmental Perception, Attitudes and Values,* Prentice-Hall, Englewood Cliffs NJ, 1974, pp.225, 248.

53 *Press,* 9 January 2012, p. A3.

54 Austin Mitchell, *The Half Gallon Quarter Acre Pavlova Paradise,* Christchurch, Whitcombe and Tombs, 1972.

55 Tuan, *Topophilia*, p.225.

56 Ibid., p.246.

57 Eric Pawson, 'Confronting Nature', in Cookson and Dunstall (eds), *Southern Capital*, p.77.

58 '2013 Census QuickStats about Greater Christchurch', Statistics New Zealand, www.stats.govt.nz/Census/2013-census/profile-and-summary-reports/quickstats-about-greater-chch (accessed 4 March 2015).

59 Ibid.

60 'Summerset – Welcome Home' [brochure], June 2015.

61 'Alpine View Lifestyle Village – Premier' [brochure], November 2014.

62 'Honouring the Prophets, The Aranui Sisters', reprinted from *The Common Good*, 23 (Lent 2002), http://www.catholicworker.org.nz/cg/CG23-Honouring.htm (accessed 14 July 2015).

Beyond the Rupture

1 Laura Borrowdale, 'The Art of Renewal', *Kia Ora*, April 2014, p.53.

2 *Metropol*, 29 May 2014, p.7.

3 Editorial, *Press*, 28 February–1 March 2015, p.A20.

4 'Editorial: Tighter deadline for earthquake proofing is welcome', *Dominion Post*, 4 September 2015, www.stuff.co.nz/dominion-post/comment/71726932/Editorial-Tighter-deadline-for-earthquake-proofing-buildings-is-welcome (accessed 23 January 2016).

5 Tina Law, 'Earthquake-prone building assessments fall short, survivor says', *Press*, 11 May 2015, www.stuff.co.nz/the-press/news/68424118/earthquakeprone-building-assessments-fall-short-survivor-says (accessed 25 July 2015).

6 *Press*, 17 October 2011, p.A5.

7 *Christchurch Mail*, 19 February 2015, p.8.

8 'Open for Business' [insert], *Press*, 16 August, 2011. It later moved back to the central city in the historic New Regent Street.

9 'Beadz Unlimited', *Press*, 5 January 2012, p.A3.

10 *Press*, 13 April 2011, p.15.

11 *Metropol*, 4 August 2011, p.34.

12 Erin Bishop, 'Socking it to Mother Nature', *Ashburton Guardian*, 1 July 2011, p.1.

13 Silty certificate document.

14 Barnaby Bennett, James Dann, Emma Johnson and Ryan Reynolds (eds), *Once*

in a Lifetime: City Building after Disaster in Christchurch, Freerange Press, Christchurch, 2014.

15 Matt Morris, 'Create gardens on vacant sections', *Press*, 7 November 2012, www.stuff.co.nz/the-press/opinion/7915329/Create-gardens-on-vacant-sections (assessed 24 January 2016); Matt Morris, 'Matt Morris says we should eat the red zone', *Press*, 17 July 2015, www.stuff.co.nz/the-press/opinion/70272139/Opinion-Matt-Morris-says-we-should-eat-the-red-zone (assessed 24 January 2016).

16 'Christchurch Icons Glorified', *Press*, 19 November, 2011, p.A11.

17 *Press*, 27 December 2011, p.A7.

18 'Women's Voices Oral History Project Launched on UC Quakestudies', University of Canterbury, www.ceismic.org.nz/news/women%E2%80%99s-voices-oral-history-project-launched-on-uc-quakestudies (accessed 25 July 2015).

19 https://Christchurchartgallery.org.nz (accessed 11 May 2013).

20 *Anglican Life*, 15 (October/November 2011).

21 Katie Pickles, 'Workers and Workplaces – Industry and Modernity', in John Cookson and Graeme Dunstall (eds), *Southern Capital: Christchurch: Towards a City Biography, 1850–2000*, Canterbury University Press, Christchurch, 2000, p.138.

22 Journalist Philip Matthews investigated the word 'munted', discovering that its meanings included 'ugly' in Scottish and Welsh, and 'being drunk' in English. 'Munter' meant 'merry' in German, and 'Munt' was also a derogatory Boer word for an African. See Philip Matthews, 'Munted Goes International', Your Weekend, *Press*, 3 September 2011, p.10.

ACKNOWLEDGEMENTS

The staff at Bridget Williams Books have been a pleasure to work with. Particular thanks to Tom Rennie for his energy, innovation and expertise, to Jane Parkin, Nancy Swarbrick and Jo Scully and to the manuscript's readers: Charlotte Macdonald, Vincent O'Malley, Geoff Walker and Bridget Williams.

Knowledge gained from my past teachers, colleagues, students and audiences at community lectures vitally informs these pages. I also thank Joanna Cobley and our wonderful summer school students and guest lecturers from 2012 to 2015 for the HIST 294/394 course 'Recovering Christchurch 1850–2010', where many of the ideas in this book were aired. Staff at the University of Canterbury's libraries are greatly appreciated.

Family and friends have offered useful research materials and appreciated childcare. Most of all, Mike McCosker has cared for Eve, Clara and James. He has also discussed history, ideas and words. In multiple ways, I am so very grateful, and this book is dedicated to him.

ABOUT THE AUTHOR

Katie Pickles is Professor and Head of History at the University of Canterbury and is Past-President of the New Zealand Historical Association. Katie graduated as a senior scholar with a double major in History and Geography from the University of Canterbury in 1989. After working as the editor of *Canta,* she undertook postgraduate study at the University of British Columbia in Vancouver, where she completed a first class MA in 1991. In 1996 her PhD was granted by McGill University in Montreal and Katie returned to Canterbury to lecture. Katie is also the author of *Transnational Outrage: The Death and Commemoration of Edith Cavell,* and *Female Imperialism and National Identity: Imperial Order Daughters of the Empire.* She has published over fifty essays, opinion editorials and journal articles on a variety of topics and has edited five collections: *New Zealand's Empire* (with Catharine Coleborne); *Endurance and the First World War: Experiences and Legacies in New Zealand and Australia* (with David Monger and Sarah Murray); *Contact Zones: Aboriginal and Settler Women in Canada's Colonial Past* (with Myra Rutherdale); *Shifting Centres: Women and Migration in New Zealand History* (with Lyndon Fraser); and *Hall of Fame: Life Stories of New Zealand Women* (with Olive Baylyn).

About BWB Texts

BWB Texts are short books on big subjects: succinct narratives spanning history, memoir, contemporary issues, science and more from great New Zealand writers. All BWB Texts are available digitally, with selected works also in paperback. New Texts are published monthly – please visit www.bwb.co.nz to see the latest releases.

BWB Texts include:

Paul Callaghan: Luminous Moments
Foreword by Catherine Callaghan

Creeks and Kitchens: A Childhood Memoir
Maurice Gee

Report from Christchurch
Rebecca Macfie

Hidden Agendas: What We Need to Know about the TPPA
Jane Kelsey

Geering and God, 1965–71: The Heresy Trial that Divided New Zealand
Lloyd Geering

Inequality and the West
Robert Wade

The Zealandia Drowning Debate: Did New Zealand Sink Beneath the Waves?
Hamish Campbell

The Quiet War on Asylum
Tracey Barnett

What Happened at Waitangi?
Claudia Orange

When the Tour Came to Auckland
Geoff Chapple

Thorndon: Wellington and Home, My Katherine Mansfield Project
Kirsty Gunn

First Contact: Tasman's Arrival in Taitapu, 1642
Anne Salmond

Wellbeing Economics: Future Directions for New Zealand
Paul Dalziel & Caroline Saunders

Growing Apart: Regional Prosperity in New Zealand
Shamubeel Eaqub